# A
# SPIRITUAL JOURNEY
# TO ENLIGHTENMENT
# GRIEF

*A Course In Miracles Awakening*

## JEANETTE SHEWCHUK

**BALBOA.**
PRESS
A DIVISION OF HAY HOUSE

This book is a work of non-fiction. Unless otherwise noted, the author and the publisher make no explicit guarantees as to the accuracy of the information contained in this book and in some cases, names of people and places have been altered to protect their privacy.

All interior images: by Jeanette Shewchuk

Cover art, the painting "An Awakening"
by Jeanette(Prysiazniuk) Shewchuk
Web site: www.jeanetteshewchuk.com.

Photography by Brad Pretula
Brad Pretula Photography
Web site: www.bradpretulaphotography.ca.

Balboa Press books may be ordered through booksellers or by contacting:

Balboa Press
A Division of Hay House
1663 Liberty Drive
Bloomington, IN 47403
www.balboapress.com
1 (877) 407-4847

Because of the dynamic nature of the Internet, any web addresses or links contained in this book may have changed since publication and may no longer be valid. The views expressed in this work are solely those of the author and do not necessarily reflect the views of the publisher, and the publisher hereby disclaims any responsibility for them.

The author of this book does not dispense medical advice or prescribe the use of any technique as a form of treatment for physical, emotional, or medical problems without the advice of a physician, either directly or indirectly. The intent of the author is only to offer information of a general nature to help you in your quest for emotional and spiritual well-being. In the event you use any of the information in this book for yourself, which is your constitutional right, the author and the publisher assume no responsibility for your actions.

Print information available on the last page.

ISBN: 978-1-9822-2482-0 (sc)
ISBN: 978-1-9822-2484-4 (hc)
ISBN: 978-1-9822-2483-7 (e)

Library of Congress Control Number: 2019903693

Balboa Press rev. date: 01/25/2020

# GRIEF

Grief is an intense emotional and mental journey during which we bind our loved ones to ourselves with heavy chains of pain, imprisoning both. There are no easy paths, no magic words can release those chains.

Slowly, methodically move forward, one step at a time. Face the dark tunnel of unbearable heartbreak. Crawl inch by inch, listen to it, taste it, feel the turmoil in your gut, spit in its face, breathe in every bit of unfinished business; the regrets, would have's, could have's, and wishing what is would be different. Keep that forward hypnotic motion, battle through thorns and all seen and unseen demons. Scream, cry, until you are exhausted! Emotionally spent!

Step out of the tunnel, stand upright, breathe in intentionally and deeply. Sense a blanket of peace enveloping your whole being, allow it to dry the tears and wipe the darkness out of your eyes, as a loving light begins to gently melt away the pain. Tuck memories of your loved one safely and lovingly away in your heart. Visit there any time you want or need unconditional love. Give and receive, but do not linger there.

Release their Spirits, grant them freedom and peace of the Light. They are never far from you, only a thought away. Honor the completion of your loved one's contract and move forward towards your Soul's intended purpose in this lifetime. Set your intentions, summon your Spiritual Helpers and begin the next important chapter of your life.

One step at a time.
**Compose your Redemption Song!**

# CONTENTS

# ACKNOWLEDGEMENTS

A tremendous amount of gratitude is extended to Jesus, for dictating *A Course in Miracles* and assisting humanity in awakening from this dream. Gratitude to Helen Schucman, for being the vessel through which Jesus' words were channelled, and William Thetford for assisting with scribing of the message. I will always be grateful to my niece, Vivian, for her generous offer to lend me a choice of books, one of which was *A Course of Miracles*.

Great gratitude to: My late-husband, Steven, for providing life situations for tremendous spiritual growth and giving me an incredible gift of Love by fulfilling his spiritual contract. My son, Warren, for honoring my requests for help in accessing information during my search for answers. My daughter, Yvonne, for assisting me with the use of a computer, providing me with a means to type the manuscript and submit it for publishing. My daughter-in-law, Wendy, for long hours spent editing the first draft. My grandchildren, Abigail and Benjamin, for being the go-to-place in my heart in remembering why it was important to write this book. My partner, Rick, for being my mirror in our personal work together toward awakening from this dream. My nephew, Brad Pretula, for coming to my rescue with his creative photography.

Great gratitude to: All my immediate and extended family, friends and everyone in my life, for providing ample opportunities to study and apply the theory of *projection and mirroring*, contributing greatly to my spiritual growth. My Soul-Group, Spirit Guides, and Jesus, for providing me with assistance, experiences, and answers throughout this journey. Without all of them, this book would not have been possible.

Thank-you!

# INTRODUCTION

I grew up on a farm in a rural area of Manitoba, Canada. I am the youngest of twelve children with an age span of 20 years between myself and my oldest surviving brother. During my formative years, I spent most of my days trying to entertain myself. I would roam nearby pastures and forested areas, walking over beaver dammed rivers and climbing trees. It was this time spent with nature, imaginary friends, and most certainly with my Guardian Angel that played a big role in nurturing the creative ability of my imagination, which contributed greatly toward self-expression through visual art.

My parents were members of the Ukrainian Greek Orthodox church. My father was a regular church goer and as children, we often accompanied him. My mother would attend also, but at times chose to stay at home. Even at a young age, I understood that it was not necessary to go to church to be in touch with one's spirituality.

I was always eager to accompany my family to Sunday service, but it was not the ceremonial rituals, nor that day's lesson that captured my interest. The small church my father helped build was covered with beautifully hand painted murals; the gift of a drifter who asked only for food, liquor, and lodging as payment.

Surrounded by these images, I would find myself transported, lost in an unworldly realm of mystical landscapes inhabited by Spirits, Saints, Angels, and, of course, Jesus. Looking absolutely amazing in colourful robes and embraced by a brilliant light, standing with arms open, lovingly inviting all to enter God's kingdom.

Little did I know that a world, which drew me into itself, would ultimately have profoundly influenced the destination of my life's journey. The hours spent breathing life into those beautiful murals conditioned my mind to be more receptive and accepting of a possibility that the world I *believed* to be real, could simply be *imagined*; the possibility that the world I thought I *imagined*, could be *real*.

As I grew older, I developed a keen interest in psychology, having spent time reading my brother's university text books, which were stored at home. Nevertheless, when I expressed interest in going to university, my parents seemed unreceptive to the idea, simply suggesting that I would soon marry and did not need to further my education. I empathized with my parents, knowing they had sacrificed much for their children and did not press the idea of university any further. I moved to the city where I spent a number of years working as a secretary, married, and was soon a-stay-at-home mom to my two children. This gave me an opportunity to nurture my love of painting, as I worked to establish a career in art.

Psychology had not abandoned me; however, since I embraced and applied its principles many times in my life, trying to understand behavior of myself and others. Often my experiences drove me to question the cruelty of life. The difficulties I was forced to overcome left me feeling that surely, *there must be a better way.* The premature and unexpected death of my husband unlocked many questions about life's deepest mysteries, and I was desperate for answers. A search for clarity led me to obtain my certification in Time-Line Therapy, which furthered my interest in the inner world of the mind.

My volunteer work with Hospice and Palliative care and as a Spiritual Visitor in a care home, gave me tremendous appreciation for gifts of wisdom accumulated through life experiences. My interest in writing was awakened during a process of preparing talks and sharing my new-found truth with members of the Spiritualist Church. Many quotes from *A Course In Miracles* are a testament to its monumental role in my spiritual journey.

The passion for writing this book is further evidence of a guided direction of my life's purpose. My initial intent was to share this important part of my life experience with my family in the hope that they, too, would come to appreciate knowledge, which nourishes my heart and Soul.

With raw honesty and openness, I share my story, hoping that you may recognize yourself in its narrative and begin your own search for truth. As you read observations and analysis of my journey, you may choose to apply those same deep and personal questions to your own life, as you travel within toward self-discovery. My book may serve to open a window in your mind through which you may choose to follow a Light casting clear vision of your True Realty, as you begin to awaken from this dream.

*"Let us today behold earth disappear at first transformed, and then, forgiven, fade entirely into God's Holy Will."*[1]

This is also my will which is God's Will. Feelings of pain, hate, guilt and death, which makes up this world, will be forever replaced with Love and Eternity at Home with God. Jesus teaches that there are many roads to an awakened Self; this book was written with sincere hope that all who seek will find their path.

---

I enjoy spending time communing with nature, while exploring the rural setting of my home along the Assiniboine River. Spirituality inspires my creativity and continues to be expressed through life. I am blessed with a wonderful loving family: a daughter, son, daughter-in-law, two grandchildren and am presently sharing my semi-retired life with my life-partner, as we all continue to journey together on a spiritual healing path.

Jeanette (Prysiazniuk) Shewchuk

# CHAPTER

# 1

# THE SCRIPT IS WRITTEN

*Life is a series of beginnings and endings.*
*Both can be just as painful.*

During our morning coffee, we discussed our trip to Swan River. Steve and Ray intended on leaving for their fishing trip either Tuesday or Wednesday morning. This would give them three to four days of fishing. Our return plans included leaving on Saturday by noon, so we would be back in Winnipeg that evening.

Steve had a day to get all his gear ready, which was plenty of time; however, he could not settle down. He was extremely restless and his thoughts were very scattered. He would jump up off his chair, with intention and purpose; then, promptly sit back down. I tried to calm his mind assuring him there wasn't a definite schedule to keep and whenever we are ready to go, we would simply leave. Nevertheless, this was not sufficient to settle his uneasiness, which continued relentlessly throughout the day.

The following morning, as we were getting ready to leave, Steve was like a caged animal unable to find his way out. He was very frustrated, seemingly angry, and so intensely agitated his whole body vibrated with tremendous stress. There was nothing I could say, or do to help him. His mind appeared to be entangled in a monumental emotional battle and any attempt to get rid of this turmoil was failing miserably. This disruptive and disturbing behavior was playing havoc with my nerves. I focused on staying out of his way in an attempt to avoid further disharmony.

As we drove out of the driveway, tension was palpable, anxiety permeated the air we were breathing, filling the interior of the truck. It was a six-hour drive to Swan River during which five and a half hours were spent in total silence. I tried to find a radio station that would relax him, but he would just tell me to turn it off. He was extremely preoccupied and distraught.

Only as we approached our destination, approximately thirty miles away, he finally spoke. He seemed to be unusually peaceful and in a surreal state. I asked him to please be careful on the fishing trip. There was intense focus on carefully chosen words, as he spoke softly and calmly in an attempt to reassure me, "There is nothing to worry about, I will be perfectly safe in a full body survival suit." I had no choice, but let that be enough to comfort me.

## LOVE OF OUTDOOR LIFE

Steve and Ray had a lot in common. They both enjoyed hunting, fishing, and outdoor activities in general. My sister and her husband, Ray, lived near the beautiful Duck Mountains, ideal for enjoying many lakes and trails. The area was full of high rolling hills not quite fitting the description of mountains, other than to people who lived mostly on flat prairie land. It was primarily unpopulated, except for plenty of wildlife and lakes filled with fish. A paradise for anyone who enjoyed the outdoors, camping, fishing, hunting, fun on all-terrain vehicles, and snowmobiling.

This was a perfect place for Steve and Ray to explore and enjoy. They experienced many trips together. One area, more frequently visited, was a remote lake named Armit Lake. The only way to get there was to travel approximately twenty miles by truck, park the truck, transfer all camping supplies onto trailers pulled by all-terrain vehicles; then, drive through bogs and wooded areas until they got to the lake. Once there, they would retrieve a boat, hidden in the bush, and load it up with all their fishing and camping gear. After all that, they continued to one of the many islands in the area. Finally; arriving at their intended destination, they would set up camp for a number of days of fishing and just enjoying life.

Steve tried to describe the scenery to me, excitedly expressing the beauty, quietness, and profound peacefulness of their favorite spot. He said that swimming was probably out of the question since the water was extremely cold in that lake. Smiling, as he added, "I'm sure the winter ice doesn't melt, it just sinks." Many times, he would mention that he'd like me to go with him one day to enjoy it as well. If it were not for circumstances, I would have been with them on that particular excursion.

Ray had called Steve several times wanting to plan one more fishing trip before winter. Steve discussed it with me; however, I felt it was important to take our grandchildren out camping once more before they went back to school. We planned a trip to Hecla Island, a beautiful provincial park.

I suggested we take the boat, but Steve was reluctant to do so. He expressed concern that Lake Winnipeg was a large lake and prone to extremely dangerous waves. As it turned out, it was, indeed, very windy and the lake seemed rather angry. In hindsight, we were glad we had not taken the boat. We spent a wonderful time biking, hiking, swimming, and enjoyed sharing around a campfire. With the last camping weekend with the grandchildren out of the way, Ray and Steve were now free to plan their outdoor adventure.

## ODD BEHAVIOR

Four months earlier, Steve and I celebrated our 40th wedding anniversary, the same way we celebrated every anniversary, working in the yard. On this particular anniversary, we planted a mystery tree in our front yard. It was a tree purchased on sale, which had lost its description tag. We guessed it was a fruit tree and thought it would be interesting to eventually find out, as it matured. Unbeknown to either of us at the time, that tree would eventually be a significant means of Spirit communication.

Upon Steve's retirement, we spent several years travelling with a truck and 5th wheel trailer. Many times, while on the highway, we encountered bad weather. I recall moments frantically searching a map to find a location of a county, for which there was a tornado or an intense weather watch. There had been numerous close calls on icy highways. I often expressed concern about not having made any plans regarding funeral arrangements. I worried about our children, one day needing to deal with a very stressful situation if we did meet our end while travelling. It was important for me to have our wishes in place, so they wouldn't have to make crucial decisions.

A few weeks before the planned fishing trip, while we were walking in a park near our home, Steve, unexpected, said to me, "I know what should be done with our bodies when we die. We should be cremated and in our memory, we could donate a bench to the park." In fact, he picked a spot at the bend of the river, overlooking a beautiful scene with a view up and down the river. We talked about proceeding with the bench and placing it exactly where we wanted it, so our children would not have to deal with any of those details.

After a few months of retirement, Steve took on a part-time job, requiring travelling two hours out of Province, there he would spend the weekend working. Before he would leave in the morning, I always made a point of kissing him good-bye and telling him I loved him. I was concerned that one day he would walk out the door, and I would not have another opportunity for a last good-bye.

## PREMONITIONS

Early in our relationship, Steve mentioned that one of his buddies had given him some profound advice for love and life, telling him it was important to withhold one's true feelings toward someone, play hard to get, to keep one on one's hook, so to speak. I did tell him what I thought about that advice, but I often wondered if he didn't frequently continue to implement that theory in his life.

Steve was not an outwardly affectionate man, in fact, he found it very difficult to be openly demonstrative not only to me, but also to his children. He seemed to show signs of mellowing with respect to his grandchildren. Perhaps he felt his sole responsibility to his grandchildren was to spoil them with affection, leaving the job of teaching life lessons to their parents. Therefore, he was more willing to open his heart, allow his feelings to flow and love freely.

A few weeks before the fishing trip, Steve's behavior seemed to take on aspects not typical of his usual routine. One particular day, as he was working in the garage, he came into the house walked directly and intentionally to where I was standing and put his arms around me. This behavior, although very much out of character, was what I desired all of our married life. I grasped his arms and hung on, cherishing the moment, reluctant to let go. He asked, "What's wrong?" I responded, "Absolutely nothing is wrong, I'm simply enjoying the moment." I tried to engrave it into memory.

Other unusual situations occurred, such as frequently walking in from working in the yard, checking on what I was doing; then, promptly going out again. Many times, he would walk in and ask a question regarding what happens when one dies. He wondered if the death of the body was the end of existence. I knew in my heart that who we really are would leave the body upon death. I always felt the dogma of organized religion was not in line with an inner knowing.

We talked about my experience at his father's funeral, while kissing his father's cheek to say good-bye, the body felt cold and clay-like in texture, completely devoid of any life. I knew that he was not in the body, and that not only was the Spirit of his father still very much alive, I had an overwhelming feeling that he was watching this whole scene.

I mentioned a conversation I had with a co-worker, who shared a personal story regarding her husband's death. She recalled witnessing a misty cloud move out of her husband's body at the moment of his death, believing it to be his Soul. Steve seemed very comforted to hear that.

I also reminded him of a near-death experience I had fifteen years earlier, which granted me amazing insights and greatly transformed my belief system. I kept expressing to him with total conviction that life continues after a body dies. Deep in my heart, I knew that the death of our body is not the end of who we really are; somehow, somewhere, we still exist. After I shared with him any and all information I had regarding death, he appeared to relax. His green eyes shone with contentment, as he returned to what he was working on.

The day before we were to leave for Swan River, Steve fell asleep on the sofa, while I was busy doing some mending. As I walked past him, I glanced down at him. His appearance stopped me in my tracks. The color of his skin was sallow and pale and it was dark, purplish brown under his eyes. His body looked completely lifeless. My heart skipped a beat, and terror slowly crept through me. I stared at his chest, watching for movement, anxiously waiting for his next breath. Finally; he took a breath!

Greatly relieved, I continued with my chores, but was left feeling completely off balance and confused by what just happened. I spent the rest of my day reprimanding myself for even briefly having a thought that he might be dead. I was repulsed and horrified by the experience and tried desperately to erase it from my mind. That situation set the tone for quiet repos, which continued into the following day.

# CHAPTER
# 2

# KEEPING BUSY - A LOT TO DO

*If you place your heart in a bubble, refuse pain and joy to enter in, you will miss an opportunity for the unfoldment of the beauty of your Soul.*

It was a relief to arrive at my sister's house, late that day. That evening, as usual, whenever Steve and Ray got together, they would visit while sampling Ray's homemade wine. They both enjoyed making wine and experimenting with different berries that grew in the area. Usually they would stay up rather late. I joined them briefly, but was exhausted by an extremely trying day, excused myself and went to bed. The stress of the day took a toll on my body, and I was emotionally, psychologically, and physically drained. I was pleasantly surprised to find that Steve, too, decided to forgo the usual late night talking and followed me to bed.

Morning arrived too soon. A restless night caused me to get up in the middle of the night and take a sleeping pill, which left me groggy and spaced out. I struggled to focus. Vicky had an early appointment at the hospital for one of her treatments. Her health was the reason I was not going on this fishing trip; I was staying behind to help her. While our husbands were having breakfast, we left to address my sister's scheduled appointment.

Vicky needed to be at the hospital for a few hours, so I decided to walk back to the house, hoping I could clear my head while enjoying the beautiful autumn morning. As I walked, feeling rather melancholy, I reflected on my favorite time of the year. Specifically, the joy of watching Mother-Nature painting her living masterpiece, flawlessly manipulating brilliant hues of color, while transforming the landscapes. The crispness of the morning air signified that change was coming. Even though, there is sadness, seeing the plants dying and leaves falling, there is a graceful acceptance of letting go of what was now past and closing that chapter. A time of rest is usually welcomed, an opportunity for spirit to be revitalized, filling one with motivation and eagerly looking forward to new growth and an awakening of new life. Clearly, at that time, I was totally oblivious of the symbolic message my thoughts were revealing to me.

Upon returning to the house, the guys were hurriedly and excitedly packing all their supplies for the fishing trip. I focused on preparing lunch for them to have before they left. After they ate, I kept myself busy cleaning the kitchen. Suddenly, I stopped; I ran as quickly as I could to the door. I was afraid they left without saying good-bye. Just then, Steve was coming back to the door. We kissed, a mid-air hurried kiss, as I said to him, "Don't do anything stupid!"

The following days were spent cleaning Vicky's house, de-cluttering, opening windows, and allowing fresh air in, providing a more conducive environment for healing. She had been ill for some time and not able to keep up with the housework.

On Saturday morning, I decided to take some luggage to the truck, so we could be ready to leave by noon. It was already a very warm sunny day, everything was absolutely still, somewhat stifling and claustrophobic, no movement of air, birds, chipmunks, or any other life. Upon reaching the truck, a wave of tremendous grief swept through me. My legs went limp. I sank to my knees, wrapping my arms around my belly, attempting to suppress intense emotional pain, as it convulsed deep in my gut. Unbearable anguish, tearing at my insides, begging release, slowly working its way out in a silent scream.

Confused and distraught, I returned to the house and tried to keep occupied, not wanting to think beyond focusing on what I was doing. Noon arrived. Steve and Ray were not back. Still reeling from my earlier inexplicable experience, worry consumed me. I moved without purpose, immersed in deep sorrow. Upon expressing my concern, Vicky dismissed my apprehension by saying they probably decided to go fishing once more before leaving for home. In my heart, I knew that was not true. I hoped she was right. I tried to convince myself they would arrive soon and continued to keep busy, desperately trying to find more things to do.

I decided to clean the dining room and started dusting the top of the china cabinet. I reached to move a framed picture of the *Sacred Heart of Jesus* and was awe struck with what I was seeing; *Jesus* looked magnificent! The whole picture glowed, it was completely encompassed by an ethereal Light, gloriously radiating from the heart of His Soul. I stared at it, surprised and enthralled, trying to comprehend what I was seeing. Slowly, I became increasingly sickened, as I remembered a particular conversation with Steve.

Several years earlier, my siblings and I sat vigil at our mother's bedside, waiting for her Spirit's passing. One of those days, while my siblings left to go to the cafeteria to get something to eat, I remained at my mother's side. As I sat with her, she, suddenly, stopped breathing. Completely taken by surprise, I was overcome with fear of the obvious; I was losing her. Panic and grief took hold of me as tears rolled down my face. I was inconsolable, not ready to let her go. Miraculously; she took a breath; then, another, once again; then, she continued to breathe.

A few days later, my sisters contemplated going for lunch, and once again, I volunteered to stay with Mom. Moments before they left, they stopped to admire a framed picture of the *Sacred Heart of Mary*, hanging on the wall beside my mother's bed. We reminisced about the fact that our brother framed it specifically for Mom and were commenting on the beautiful job of his workmanship as they proceeded to walk out of the room.

While continuing to admire the picture, I found myself becoming eerily transfixed and spellbound by what was unfolding in front of my eyes. *Mary* was transforming into a heavenly vision, as a celestial luminescence slowly moved through her, exquisitely bathing the picture entirely in mystical light, gradually fading as it travelled beyond. I gazed with wonder and delight and was utterly dumbstruck at how that was possible. I looked down at my Mom and, only then, became aware that she had passed away. I was convinced that it was her Spirit that moved into and through the picture as it journeyed into the unknown. Her choosing to leave this way, softened the pain of losing her. I was able to let her go. I quietly sang her favorite song, *"Irene goodnight ..... I will see you in my dreams."*

After sharing the experience of my mom's Spirit moving into and through the picture of the *Sacred Heart of Mary*, I mentioned to Steve how comforting it was to me. Was the picture of the *Sacred Heart of Jesus*, a way for Steve to let me know that he, too, had left? It would be just like Steve to choose to do the same, letting me know gently. Silently, agonizing pain of immense loss continued to engulf me.

Supper time was fast approaching, we busied ourselves preparing supper, though neither of us was hungry. I spent most of the time, trying to process being weirdly aware of Ray and Steve's *presence. They* were with us in the kitchen, hearing our conversation. Supper was put away untouched. I asked Vicky to call someone she may know that would go to look for the guys. She kept reassuring me that they were okay, they were probably having such a good time they decided to stay a few days longer.

## THE SCENE WAS SET

As proof it was possible for them to choose to stay a few days longer, Vicky relayed a situation to me, which had happened only a couple of weeks earlier. Ray had gone camping and fishing by himself and was suppose to arrive home on a certain day. When he did not arrive home as expected, Vicky panicked and asked some of his friends to look for him; she was worried he had encountered an unforeseen problem. When he finally did arrive home, safe and sound, he made it clear to her that she was never to do that again. He had been having a great time and simply decided not to return home on the day he originally planned.

I knew that Steve would never have done that to me, especially knowing how worried I had been about him going in the first place. He always kept his word, unless it was impossible to do so. The turmoil I felt, the constant churning in the pit of my stomach, continued relentlessly.

The next day, Sunday, I attacked the living room, cleaning, dusting and washing, knowing I needed to keep busy to save my sanity. I spent most of the time trying to resist a persistent feeling of immeasurable loss from completely consuming me. I kept telling myself, focus, focus, don't think, don't think. If ever an - in the now - moment occurred in my life, it was then.

Supper time came and went, once again, I begged Vicky to call someone. She said if they weren't home by eight o'clock, she would call Ray's friend. Eight o'clock arrived. She made the phone call. The friend told her that because it was getting late and dark, he would set out in the morning. I had to try and survive the night. Worried sick hardly described my state of mind.

# IT IS WHAT IT IS!

I slept in the basement bedroom, and Vicky slept in her bedroom upstairs. After spending what seemed like hours of desperately trying to sleep, I heard the door bell ring and my sister getting up to answer the door. I panicked, thinking, "She shouldn't answer the door in the middle of the night." I practically flew up the stairs trying to get there as quickly as my legs could carry me.

When I got to the door, R.C.M.P. officers were walking in. Standing behind them, I could see Steve in his full survival suit carrying his fishing-line and tackle box. My heart skipped a beat. I breathed a sigh of relief, as I thought to myself, "Oh, thank goodness, he's okay." The look on his face was saying, "Boy, am I in trouble now," and I was thinking, "You've got that right."

The door was promptly closed on him. I could hear the police say to Vicky, "We need someone to identify the other gentleman. Here is his photo." I refused to look at the photo, insisted that Steve was just outside the door and demanded they let him in. I heard Vicky say, "That's my brother-in-law, Steve." I protested loudly, "It can't be, he's just outside!" I tried to push past the police, but they held me back and would not let me open the door.

My life slammed into a brick wall. From that moment forward events of the night moved, as though, through dense dark fog. Words sounding deliberate and methodical; information coming slowly and painfully. Muffled rumblings gradually fading into silence, rapidly developing into my worst nightmare.

My sister's friends stayed with us, trying to console us and keep us occupied with idle chatter, attempting to introduce some faction of normalcy into the room. As I sat on the living room couch in a shocked and numb state, I could clearly see the picture of the *Sacred Heart of Jesus*, where I had left it on top of the dining room cabinet. Still glowing and shimmering with a luminous light, shining eminently brighter than before, as it gently and lovingly smiled at me. It was drawing me in, wanting to console me; I understood. Steve's Spirit was letting me know he was very much alive and was there to comfort and provide me with much needed courage. I believe that knowing, was what gave me the strength to phone my children.

The next morning, Vicky's friends began dropping in to offer comforting words and condolences. One of her friends was also an old friend of mine. As he was leaving, he gently put his arms around me and held me briefly. At that very moment, I became completely overwhelmed by Steve's essence and presence, as he whispered in my ear, "I wish I could be there for you."

## A DIFFERENT LIFE - NOW REALITY

The next day, it was brought to our attention that the friend who was called on that fateful Sunday evening, already knew Steve and Ray were not coming home. He and his son had gone out to that area on Sunday morning, to set things up for hunting season when they discovered the half-submerged boat and one of the bodies near the shore.

Because of the remote area and difficulty in transporting the bodies, it took police all day to get there and come back. We didn't know what happened, or even when it happened. All we knew was that the boat was half-submerged and the bow was sticking up above the water. The motor was missing. Steve's body was found not too far from the boat. Ray's body was a mile away with one boot missing. Both were wearing their full body survival suits. The date of their deaths was recorded as September 14, the day their bodies were found. I felt in my heart it was around the time when I took the luggage to the truck, the 13th, the morning they were to arrive home.

It was possible they had decided to go for one more morning of fishing, but we will never really know for sure. The R.C.M.P. report didn't have any explanation, as to what might have happened, merely describing it as a boating accident. Autopsy reports concluded death by drowning. The water was extremely cold and even though they were wearing full body survival suits, water entered through the bottom of the suits and hyperthermia set in. Steve's heart simply stopped beating. It was what it was! That became a phrase I frequently used from then on, just to keep me moving forward on auto pilot.

My children drove to Swan River to gather Steve's things, load up the A.T.V. and help me return home. When we arrived home, I stood at the window and just stared out at the back yard. My thoughts of despair were interrupted by what was taking place in front of my eyes. The yard was literally moving with squirrels everywhere. I had a hard time believing what I was seeing. I whispered, "Steve, I know you are here, thank-you for letting me know." You see, Steve hated squirrels and was on an endless and determined quest to get rid of every last one of them. He refused to admit it was a losing battle, or to recognize that every squirrel he relocated, raced him back to our yard and got there before he returned. What better way of getting my attention, if not by orchestrating a multi-generational squirrel reunion in our back yard!

## RETURNED TO THEIR LIVES

Funeral arrangements needed to be made, too many decisions necessitated consideration, sleep was not an option, nor was grieving. Families required to travel six hours for one funeral; then, travel six hours back for another.

A whirlwind of caring friends expressing their heartfelt sympathies occupied the first few weeks following the funerals. Then, came the silence. The awful, awful silence! The reality of being completely alone with my thoughts and pain. After the funeral, my children had to get back to their jobs and their own families, returning to their lives as normally as remotely possible. Grieving when they had some time, but blessed with needing to be busy.

For me, there was just silence, regret, and knowing the past could not be changed. Most of the time was spent crying. I often described my pain, as if my chest was ripped open by a pack of hungry wolves, insidiously, relentlessly gnawing and shredding my heart. The pain was not going anywhere; there was no release. I was attempting to console my whole being, my Soul. There was nothing important, nothing I felt like doing, absolutely no desire to move. I hated myself for what I had failed to do and the many words that were left unspoken. My heart was broken, by me.

I gazed out my bedroom window at the river which ran at the back of our yard, feeling completely despondent. A thought kept going through my head, "It would be so very easy to end this pain, this horrible and unbearable pain." The next morning, while I was awakening from a brief, but much needed sleep, I very clearly heard my husband's voice saying to me, "*You must continue down your path, I will see you when you cross over.*"

I phoned a pastor, offered by my husband's work place and begged him to give me something to sustain me and help me move forward. He came to see me and handed me a booklet of psalms. As I was slowly flipping through it, feeling greatly disappointed, I said to him, "This is it?" He looked at me sympathetically; then, said, "Yeah, I know, I'm going through a really hard time myself."

## SPIRIT COMFORTING

I had many dreams, which seemed so real. I'm convinced they were true Spirit visitations. *In the first one, I saw Steve enveloped in a misty fog as he walked towards me. I ran up to him and hugged him; I felt his strong arms around me, as I excitedly express how happy I was to see him. He appeared emotionless, distant, almost like he was in shock. I asked, "Could we continue to travel together?" He said, "How?" I replied, "Why, we always travelled together, in our truck." We both climbed into the truck and were about to travel somewhere. I was overcome with such joy and filled with incredible happiness; then, I woke up.* I was deeply saddened that the dream had not continued, but for the time being, it had to be enough to somewhat console me.

I had too many regrets to count. I was sorry for the many times I had resorted to anger in our 40 years of marriage. I regretted I had not been more patient, more understanding, and that I had not loved him unconditionally. I regretted the many things left unsaid. Most importantly, that I had not given him a proper kiss goodbye and never told him I loved him, the last opportunity I had. A regret I tried to prevent from ever having, all our married life. I cried out loud and kept repeating all this, wishing for another opportunity to do so.

I sat on the edge of my bed crying and proclaiming all of this, over and over, "I didn't even give you a proper kiss goodbye!" Suddenly, I noticed the bedroom door swinging wildly back and forth, creaking loudly as it did so. I stopped crying and looked at the door, quietly observing for a few minutes before calling out, "Is that you, Steve?" The door stopped moving. Was it Steve? That only spurred more crying and begging for another opportunity to kiss him and tell him how much I loved him.

Another day went by and another restless and sleepless night. *After, at last, falling asleep for a while, I turned to lie on my right side and found Steve lying beside me. I was ecstatic! He kissed me on my lips; it was a beautiful, warm, soft kiss. It was so real! It was real! I said, "I love you" and he responded, "I love you, too." I placed my head on his chest and fell into the deepest, most peaceful, and profound sleep I ever had.* When I awoke, he wasn't there. He was gone. I expressed immense gratitude for an opportunity for one final kiss and one final goodbye. My heart felt an enormous amount of relief and peace. I was in awe that Steve, from the Spirit world, was able to do that for me; he, his Spirit, or whatever he was now, was very much alive!

Nevertheless, my grieving continued. I tried to stop crying; however, tears continue to fall. I kept the television on for noise, wanting to interrupt the eerie quiet of the house, but it was the noise in my head I truly wished to silence. One day, as I walked past the television, I heard something that caught my attention. It was on a PBS station and Wayne Dyer was speaking. I sat down, quietly watching and listening for two hours, completely absorbed in what he was saying. His words seemed to keep repeating in my head. I, greatly desired to change the way I looked at things. I was desperately wanting the pain gone, and my bleak life to be different. How could I change the way I look at things, so that the things I look at, would change?

This planted a seed in my mind, birthing an undertaking of a journey. I was suddenly fueled by an incredible boost of energy, driving a powerful need to awaken hidden knowledge. I would never have imagined in my wildest dreams where this journey would lead me.

Memorial Bench

# CHAPTER

# 3

# MANY QUESTIONS NEED ANSWERS

*"It's your road and yours alone. Others may walk with you, but no one can walk it for you."*

## RUMI

Numerous books written by Wayne Dyer were bought and read, paragraphs were underlined, and pages tagged for future reference. I had a fascination with all books regarding near-death experiences and mediumship. It was important to have affirmation that the experiences I had were genuine. Acknowledgement that many sane people had similar experiences was essential to convince me I was not delusional. The television show *Crossing Over* with *John Edwards* was regularly and faithfully watched. It brought me much joy to know that others had been in touch with loved ones who had *crossed over*. I especially needed to keep knowledge alive and well in my heart that a part of us, indeed, does exist after our bodies die. Most importantly, that the connection with our loved ones is never broken, and they are aware of our everyday lives.

On January 19, four months after Vicky and I became widows, our older sister, Nettie, also joined our prestigious club. Her husband died of a massive heart attack, another funeral required travelling. The business of arranging a funeral and receiving long lines of friends and family paying their respect and extending condolences, occupies a fair amount of time. In a strange way; however, it all becomes a welcomed distraction. Those who grieve, seem to be in a hypnotic state, doing what needs to be done without any clear thought or desire to think. My sister was in a state of disbelief, trying to compute what is taking place. When I asked Nettie if she was going to be okay after everyone left, she responded, "Oh yes." I had my reservations, knowing what was to hit her like a ton of bricks, once she was all alone with her *now reality.*

A week later, during a terrible ice storm, she called and pleaded with me to drive out to be with her. She was in a bad emotional state. I had always been a reluctant and fearful driver even at the best of times. Several six-hour trips earlier in the fall to help Vicky, somewhat, hardened my nerves. I knew how Nettie must be feeling, and I could not let her go through it alone. Having been on that same highway of life, only a few miles ahead of her, I was aware of the heart wrenching pain she was experiencing. So, I asked my Guides to keep me safe, as I faced my own fears and set off to be with her, on a treacherous four-hour drive.

I spent a week with Nettie, addressing some banking necessities and trying to provide love and moral support. With my own grief still very raw, each day I dressed warmly and went for long walks on the country road. I listened to Deepak Chopra on my mp3 player and spent time crying out to God, wanting desperately to gain strength and sustenance. I urgently needed help, so I could continue holding up not only myself, but also Nettie. I asked for strength to lift her up and give her the courage to face her now very different future. Nettie returned to the city with me to spend time with her sons before having to go back to address selling the farm and dealing with relocating.

## STANDING TALL IN GRACE

That winter, my grandchildren came to spend a weekend with me and my daughter. We spent time outside, making a snowman and dressing him up in their Gedo's cowboy hat, trying not to miss him terribly. When we went indoors to have hot chocolate and a snack, I stood at the window and stared out into the back yard. We live next to a naturalized park and a lot of wild life would often venture onto our yard. As I looked out the window,

I watched, as at least twenty five deer walked onto the yard, stood side by side and formed a semi-circle facing me. I, quickly, called the children to come and look. We were in awe of the focus and attention directed toward us. After several minutes, they broke formation, walked in a single file towards the snowman, nodding their heads as they approached him; then, continued to walked on by. I knew emphatically that Steve had orchestrated this show, to let us know that he was aware of what we were doing.

My grief had to be put on hold, and my attention continued to be redirected towards my sisters. Several more trips were made to Swan River to help Vicky proceed with her plans to relocate and be closer to her daughters. Her house had to be prepared for sale. I spent weeks with her de-cluttering years of accumulation. Even though I had moved four times in my life, de-cluttered and gotten rid of a lot of stuff with every move, I continued to collect more. It is especially noticeable, when you lived in the same house for years, how much stuff one holds on to. Once the house was sold, I was back there to help her pack her things and move to her new home in the city.

## MYSTERY TREE DELIVERS

One of the many times I was away helping Vicky, I phoned my daughter at home. She said to me, "Mom you should see that mystery tree you and Dad planted last year on your anniversary; it's completely covered in blossoms and it is beautiful!" Our forty-first anniversary would have been on that very day. Knowing that Steve was responsible for the timing of this message of love, lifted my spirit immensely.

After relocating Vicky to her new home in the city, I, once again, made the long journey back to help Nettie. She had sold her farm and needed help preparing for an auction, packing up her belongings and relocating to the city, moving forward with the new chapter of her life.

The interruptions in my grieving process were preventing me from dealing with my grief; however, I knew that I could not continue to avoid it. Time is supposed to heal all, but apparently what it did for me was just give me a bit of a reprieve from intense inner pain. Grief was still stalking me, like a wild animal, and I was terrified of facing it. I had no choice, but to face my loss, more importantly, face the demons from my past and deal with my emotional pain and regrets. I needed to tame all of it, learn to understand, forgive, and love it, so it no longer threatened me.

I reached out to anyone I thought might be able to show me how to do it. I was directed to a grief outreach program, which was limited to someone phoning and listening, while I poured out my heart's pain. There was no permanent solution to help dissolve my grief, just some tools or perhaps distractions, to make life more tolerable. I went to grief group meetings, only to find myself wanting so much more than what was offered. The saying, *time heals,* was not enough. What I wanted was directions to a road that would heal not only my grief, but all life's pain. I needed to make sense of a nightmarish existence; I wanted a different way of living in this world. It was important for me to change the way I looked at things, so that the things I looked at, changed.

## SEEING MY HUSBAND'S SPIRIT

*"The boundaries which divide life and death are at best shadowy and vague who is to say where one ends and the other begins."*[1]

I spent most of my evenings usually reading until I got tired, since sleep was still rather elusive. One evening, while I was reading one of my many books with the television on to keep me company, I dozed off. *As I stirred in a semi-sleep state, I clearly saw my husband, dressed in his favorite well-worn sweat pants and sweater, walking out of the bedroom. Excitedly, I said, "Steve is that you?" Immediately, his physical image disappeared.* In a semi-sleep, deeply relaxed state, my vibrations were raised and I was able to tap into a higher dimension. Even though his energy was still in the room, it was my intense emotional reaction that very quickly lowered my vibration and greatly diminished my ability to visually maintain that connection.

# WHAT THOSE ON THE THRESHOLD
# OF DEATH TEACH US

*"The best way to find yourself is to lose yourself in the service of others."*[2]

My daily walking continued to give me an opportunity to listen to audio books. As I searched for answer to many questions, I began to form a belief system, which included a certainty that our true essence is eternal, and there is no such thing as *sin* or *hell*. It was also becoming apparent to me that if one believes in either of those things, they could be very real to them. A belief is created in the mind; therefore, it would seem that one's beliefs could be changed simply by changing one's mind. One would surely think so; however, I soon was to find out, it wasn't that easy.

Increasingly, I felt a need to be of value, to make my life worthwhile. I decided to volunteer in a nursing home. This service was to be in the capacity of a spiritual visitor to those who had no friends, or loved ones to spend time with them. The intent was to bring them some company, conversation, and perhaps some happiness. I soon recognized that what I thought I was giving them, was in fact, the other way around. A deep sense of peace and love was experienced during these visits. I felt honored to be in the presence of beings filled with tremendous life's lessons and wisdom. While driving home, most often than not, my companions would be love and peace.

Those approaching the end of their lives would often share some of their learned life lessons, the greatest one of these learned, or in some cases missed, was that the only important thing to accomplish in life is to love. Everything else is insignificant and completely valueless. It was apparent that regrets, a need for forgiving others and most importantly oneself, was foremost in their minds.

A question that often brought deep thought, was, "What would you have not learned if you hadn't had the life that you had?" We would talk about why things might have happened the way they did, what they could learn from it, and to try to find it in their hearts to forgive. Everyone needs peace in knowing that who they really are never dies and upon leaving their earthly bodies, they will be going Home. There they will be reunited with greatly missed loved ones who passed on before them. Instead of regrets, guilt and blame, we should be extremely grateful, for an opportunity to learn from a life's situation, a gift for our Soul.

## WANTING TO HELP OTHERS WHO GRIEVE

I took a course in Hospice and Palliative Care, wanting to share my rapidly evolving truth, hoping that it could help others with their grief. During this course, which was a week of informative interactive teaching in a group setting, our seating arrangements were constantly changed to give us an opportunity to meet other people. I found myself seated next to the same woman three times in a row, which was unusual. We, of course, struck up a conversation and discussed our personal experiences with grief and dying. During this time, she mentioned a Time-line Therapy course she was taking, which proved to be beneficial in healing emotional trauma. It sounded interesting to me. I wrote down some contact information and filed it away. I was not ready for that path, just yet.

I spent some time working with those who were recently widowed; however, it wasn't long before it became apparent to me that helping others was not as simple as sharing what had worked for me. Those who were ready to grasp information I shared with them, found it to be just what they needed at that particular time. When this knowledge was eagerly embraced, it assisted them in breaking free from chains of grief and sorrow more quickly, allowing them to move forward with their lives. I respect that we are all on different paths; the choices we make along the way create necessary and appropriate opportunities for our learning, when we are ready.

## NO STRANGER TO GRIEF

I was not a stranger to grief. Over the years, I had lost my grandparents, parents, two sisters, two brothers, a nephew, two brother-in laws, my husband's parents, his brother, a sister-in-law, many aunts, uncles, cousins, along with numerous friends. The funeral home was starting to be too uncomfortably familiar.

At that time in my life, there was a necessity of having to continue with day to day life. I didn't have the time to dwell on loss, nor did I have desire to search more deeply into the mysteries of life and death. I just knew in my heart that religious beliefs were at times difficult to embrace as truth. This belief encompassed an idea that the body and personality remain in the grave until the second coming of Christ, at which time, the dead will rise up from the graves. I struggled to understanding how that was possible. Of course, cremation was not an option.

I felt this belief system held a potential to cause incredible pain in those who lost loved ones, especially children. While watching my family at the grave sites, weeping and greatly saddened, I knew the ones they were grieving for were not in the cold ground; they were beside us, trying to comfort and communicate with us. I have since concluded that the one we really grieve for the most is ourselves. The lives we lived before our loss, changed dramatically. A part of us also dies; we will never be that same person again. That life has ended, a new one begins without our loved ones.

In the spring of the following year, my oldest brother was diagnosed with cancer. Even though I was twenty years younger than he, I was determined to help him understand and become aware of what to expect. Most importantly, not to be anxious, or fearful when he was given the prognosis of only a few months to live. I lent him all kinds of books on death and shared personal experiences that I had with my late husband's Spirit.

He suffered with his illness until December. One very cold night, my sister-in-law called to tell me that he may not make it through the night. I had already crawled into bed, and since I lived out of town, the thought of having to drive in the bitter cold, made me want to cover my head with the quilt and not move. My sister-in-law informed me that she had a ride to the hospital and would spend the night there. So, I, in my mind, asked my brother to please hang on until morning. That night I had a lucid dream, it was very real.

# SPIRIT VISITATION

At first, I was baffled by what I was seeing; I watched intently, as a translucent entity, emitting a blinding light, approached me. As it moved closer, I recognized Steve, looking absolutely mystical. He beamed with such happiness; he was totally ecstatic.

He excitedly said, *"I need to tell you how wonderful it is here. It is amazing! There are majestic trees, towering mountains, and breathtaking landscapes spreading beyond endless space. Massive amounts of flowers, like hand-crafted jewels in pure and brilliant colours, blooming continuously. Everything magnified a million times in vibrancy and wonderment.*

*You would be completely in awe, as you try to comprehend what you are seeing. Its beyond anything that words could describe. The abilities - one can do anything one desires; I can even play the violin!"*

He always loved the sound of the violin and when I tried to persuade him to take lessons and learn how to play it, he would only laugh at the ridiculousness of such a suggestion. *He went on to try to express to me how extremely joyful, loving and peaceful it was there.*

I, on the other hand, was actually getting *extremely annoyed!* He is so happy and having a such a wonderful time, while I was stuck here, trying not to be *extremely miserable!* I said to him, *"Don't you miss me?"* He just smiled with such love, kindness, and understanding, and said:

*"Oh right. You don't understand! It's only a moment in time!"*

The next morning, I couldn't wait to get to my brother's bedside to tell him what was waiting for him. When I got there he was still conscious, but was no longer communicating. I held his hand and told him about Steve's visit, looked into his eyes and reassured him that it was all true and not to be afraid of where he was going. He held on to life until my other sisters arrived. Together, we helped him to go to the Light.

I was so grateful to be able to be there for him. I had a deep regret for not ever telling him how much I loved him. When I spoke with my sister-in-law, I mentioned that fact and expressed great remorse for missing many opportunities to tell him. She reassured me that he knew I loved him. *A few nights later, he visited me in my dream. I saw him walking out of a misty white cloud, directly towards me. I ran to hug him, and I told him I loved him. He responded, that he loved me too. His Spirit had an opportunity to heal my mind, and I am extremely grateful.*

# CHAPTER

# 4

# THE UNCONSCIOUS MIND

*"Why do you stay in prison when the door is wide open?
There is a candle in your heart, ready to be kindled.
There is a void in your Soul, ready to be filled. You feel
it, don't you?"*

## Rumi

I was aware we repeat the cycle of life and death and became curious about my past lives. I was interested in knowing how they may be influencing my present life. I recalled my introduction to the concept of Time-Line Therapy, a year or so earlier, and entertained possibly using that method to investigate my past lives. I found the phone number that I had filed away and proceeded to call for more information. This led to an appointment for a personal Time-Line Therapy session. I was certainly not prepared for the insights I was about to receive, nor the vast amount of understanding I would gain, regarding the primary driver of my life experience.

As we proceeded with the mild trance induction, my conscious mind kept an ongoing monologue of thoughts that were denying the whole process of hypnosis. It was convinced that hypnosis was not having any effect. Once I got deeper into past events of my life, I wasn't so sure anymore there wasn't a part of my mind that was, indeed, aware of what was happening. We visited the time of my husband's passing, and found there was an understanding and an acceptance with no residual issues requiring healing.

The therapist proceeded to take me back to the time of my birth and beyond into my mother's womb, at which point, I was completely surprised when tears started running down my face. Uncontrollable sobbing followed as acute emotional pain rose to the surface. When I was asked, "What was happening?" I cried, "My mother never wanted me, she tried to abort me."

The therapist proceeded to help my unconscious mind understand why there was such emotional pain attached to this event, so I would let it go and embrace an understanding instead. I, immediately, understood why my mother was not wanting this birth. I was, after all, my mother's twelfth pregnancy. I was fully aware that my mother worked very hard on the farm, along with my father, to provide for their nine surviving children. The thought of one more child would, certainly, have brought feelings of wishing the pregnancy did not exist.

Whether this was indeed a physical attempt to abort, or simply thoughts of not wanting the pregnancy, it didn't matter, my unconscious mind understood it to mean that *I was not wanted*, and *I was not loved*. My therapist helped me work through the healing and letting go of any possible residual negative emotions regarding my mother. I had not been aware of the existence of this inner pain; this memory was repressed in my unconscious mind.

### *"The wound is the place the light enters you."*[1]

Upon arriving home, my mind was filled with an immense amount of clarity. There wasn't the usual heavy and dense confusion of burdened thoughts that had been previously lodged in my mind. The healing effect of the Time-Line Therapy was phenomenal. The next day, an exhilarated state inundated my whole being. Tremendous elation and freedom filled me with bliss. I literally danced like no one was watching and it felt amazing, completely liberating! So much so, that I was convinced that this experience was a quick way to release unconscious past pain and heal old wounds. I wanted to share my new-found freedom and considered taking the Time-Line Therapy course, so I could help others.

## SEARCH FOR LOVE

*"Your task is not to seek for love, but merely to seek and find all the barriers within yourself that you have built against it."*[2]

By now, I understood that before we are born into this world, we decide what it is we hope to achieve in this lifetime. We choose: the type of body, our parents, siblings, financial status, geographic locations, circumstance of birth, and much more to facilitate our desired learning. The Spirit, to be my mother, whose natural true state is Love, agreed to do a very unloving thing in providing me with the psychological circumstance of a false belief that I was unloved and unwanted, to set the theme for my life's learning.

I do not recall my mother ever hugging me, or expressing love towards me. My older sisters took care of me when I was a baby, and as a young child my many attempts to be part of my mother's life *appeared* to be rejected. I wanted so much to be with my mother, following her around, trying to be helpful. In the garden, I would ultimately end up pulling out a vegetable rather than a weed and eating more peas than I put in the bucket. In the chicken coop, I would try to collect the eggs, only to accidently drop and break some of them.

In retrospect, it was understandable that I was promptly told to leave; I was more of an annoyance in her very busy life. Always being sent away, caused me to *feel* not wanted; evidently, that's how my young mind perceived it. My father was more attentive to me, since mother's patience appeared to be greatly taxed. I loved my mother dearly and certainly, now, have a greater appreciation for her thinking at that time. She would have been overwhelmed, her patience level extremely low, and she was tired. It didn't mean she didn't love me, I just *perceived* it to be so.

My sisters, eventually found me to be a pest and wanted their own space. I often wandered off into wooded areas with my imaginary friends, spending most of my days with birds and animals that inhabited the countryside. I thrived with Mother-Nature's love, whose arms are very much still a place of great comfort for me, even today. The perceived aloneness nurtured me, molded me, fed my imagination, and creativity.

I do recall my mother praising me for being a very good berry picker. There was a family owned hay field covered with wild strawberry plants, and it was a yearly excursion to pick strawberries to be preserved for winter. Encouraged by my mother's praise and, of course, wanting and needing more of it, I would dedicate myself to filling my little cup with berries, as quickly as possible, and proudly running to dump it into my mother's bucket. Then, I would stop and wait for her smile of approval, as though I was dying of thirst and needed her smile to sustain me.

Throughout my adult years, I remained attentive and empathetic to her needs. One particularly memorable moment occurred when we had been visiting and were leaving to go back to Winnipeg. My family was never very demonstrative, no one kissed or hugged. My in-laws on the other hand, were very much a huggy and kissy family. Becoming aware of the discrepancy, I decided to show my love for my family and surprised my parents by kissing them goodbye.

As I was about to close the door, I heard my mother say to my dad, "I always knew she was different." That statement stayed with me; although, I never fully understood it. It may have been the acceptance that my inner child desperately craved. It was gracefully embraced and tucked away deep in my heart for safe keeping. I am very grateful to my mother for upholding and fulfilling her sacred contract with me.

This belief of *not wanted, not loved* shaped who I thought I was, always looking for love and approval, trying to find it in the world rather than in myself. I loved my husband dearly and could never understand why he had a difficult time showing, or returning that love to me. I know now that he also was part of my Soul contract. My self-esteem and self-love was extremely lacking.

Ultimately, my journey was to take me inward to find that love, so that my life would not be controlled by looking for love outside of me. The personality I related to as being *me*, was badly tainted with many untruths, unconscious guilt, and karma accumulated from many lifetimes. It was important for me to first love myself before I could see love elsewhere. My outside world; then, would reflect my inner world. That light of understanding opened a window of knowledge, which had not existed before, expanding my overall perception of this world.

# TIME LINE THERAPY

**"Every experience, no matter how bad it seems, holds within it a blessing of some kind. The goal is to find it."** [3]

I registered for a Time-line Therapy course. This included an understanding of the unconscious mind, opening another dimension to my awareness. I obtained my NLP Practitioner, Hypnotherapy and Time Line Therapy certification. This gave me an understanding of human behaviours, drivers, and blocks that exist within everyone. As a fully qualified therapist, I was able to go ahead and assist others in liberating their minds of unresolved past traumas.

Phobias are good examples of how the unconscious mind works. During a traumatic event, the mind may choose to block out that memory completely. Most times, it simply represses the memories, but holds on to the emotions. It chooses the best way to react at a particular time to ensure the survival of a body and mind.

The reaction and the emotional pain of that experience remains in the unconscious mind. Every time a similar situation occurs, or slight variations of it, one continues to react the same way, not fully understanding why. The unconscious mind, once again, believes it is protecting you, and since that action proved to be effective before, it continues to implement that same behavior, repeatedly. At some point, that behavior starts to become a detriment to your well being, causing disharmony, disruption, and even chaos in your life.

Perhaps you or your loved ones have an innate fear of flying. One could speculate there may have been an experience of tremendous trauma, possibly dying in a plane crash in a previous life-experience. One is not conscious of that event and cannot understand the cause of the phobia. Initially not flying was a great way to avoid dealing with that fear and emotional trauma and, of course, this avoidance would prevent that same trauma from happening again. Nevertheless, not flying may diminish the quality of life. The tactic of avoidance is no longer helpful; it is preventing you from living your life fully. Residual effects from that initial trauma may also be overlapping unconsciously onto other aspects of your life.

Carrying this analogy further, if you drowned in an previous life, you may have tremendous fear of water in this lifetime. If you have been robbed, emotionally hurt in a relationship, or in any other way when faced with a potentially similar situation, the same intense emotional reaction will follow. This leaves one vulnerable to repeat these reactive patterns. Because the memory is repressed, you are not aware of the triggers that are responsible for that behavior.

The mind presents many opportunities to heal emotional suffering. What you resist will persist, until you address it by facing it, walking through it and healing that particular trauma. Until then, it will rear its ugly head over and over again. This would be creating havoc in your life, not only in repetitive self-abusive behavior, but would eventually manifest as a disease in the body. As you travel through life, those behaviours or reactions, begin to stall and even stop forward momentum of the Soul's progression.

In the process of Hypnotherapy, the unconscious mind is assisted in bringing those memories and emotions to the forefront, guided to an understanding of why the situation happened and what can be learned from it. One discovers that it is more beneficial to accept and embrace the learning rather than hold on to emotional and mental pain. There is a change in behaviors and same triggers no longer are as prominent as in the past. The repeated old patterns that have kept one entangled in a life of reactive behaviors are released. Upon healing and releasing past mental trauma there is a sense of tremendous relief and liberation, a lightening of spirit and a new approach to one's life's journey.

## JOURNEY THROUGH THE UNCONSCIOUS MIND

The unconscious is a device of the mind used as a reservoir or file in which all ideas, thoughts, feelings, and memories are filed away. Generally, they are memories that are suppressed and repressed because they are too painful to deal with; however, they are always seeking to express themselves. A person is not aware of any of these until some of them manifest in dreams and in what would appear to be dissociated acts in one's life. It is imperative for the mind to heal all these painful memories in order to become whole again. An article in *Encyclopaedia Britannica* mentions *Sigmund Freud's* observations regarding hypnosis as being useful with assisting in recalling an experience, which had been repressed and unconscious.[4]

Human beings appear to be reluctant to dive into their inner minds perhaps too frightened by what they may find. Most people are afraid they are going to find out they are as bad as they believe they are. In truth, that is opposite of what actually happens. They discover that they aren't responsible for what occurred. They obtain a tremendous amount of insights from a situation and learn to embrace amazing love and goodness that is innately within them. Their hearts open to receiving a connection to others, happiness and peace follows, as they work toward being whole once again. Those who have had enough of life's crises find this form of therapy extremely helpful.

My intention was to help heal minds of the unconscious *wrong* thinking, beliefs, and behaviours. In lieu of payment, I asked that they pay it forward. Attempting, in a very small way, to exchange pain with love within this world. At that time in my life, I was not fully aware of how humanity equates *value* with *money*. If something is offered for free, it can't possibly be as valuable as a product or service, for which there is a monetary cost. This belief is part of all other sick thinking that is within the mind.

It is a wrong belief system that continues to sustain and maintain a misconception within the mind, regarding value. It prevents the mind from seeking free help, which could heal and eliminate that wrong thinking that is creating the misconception of value in the first place. The ego's belief system prevents healing of that mind. This ego world is set up in such a way it could be nearly impossible to step off the treadmill of the birth and death cycle until one is knocked down to one's knees and cries, "There must be a better way."

Humanity has a tendency to simply accept status quo and continue going through life feeling miserable, unloved, unhappy, and unforgiving. We, either do not desire change, or lack strength and fortitude to create change. If nothing is done to modify this way of thinking in your current life, odds are pretty good you will be back in another lifetime still trying to change wrong beliefs and behaviours you were meant to address and heal during this particular lifetime.

# CHAPTER

# 5

# COMMUNICATION FROM THE SPIRIT WORLD

*"Goodbyes are only for those who love with their eyes, because for those who love with their heart and Soul, there is no such thing as separation."*

RUMI

During my Time-line Therapy course, I reconnected with the woman I met at the Hospice and Palliative Care course. She mentioned to me that her sister had successfully channelled her deceased son. Synchronicity, once again, at work. I decided to call her sister to make an appointment, hoping to communicate with my late husband.

About a year after this communication, I also was able to tap into the realm. I am aware of many techniques that are needed and implemented for communication with Spirit. Sometimes, there are symbols and metaphors that the medium needs to interpret, or there are clear voices, sensations, or images that may also appear, as a thought in one's imagination. Along with thought-transfer communication, connections are successfully made to Spirits with whom one wishes to communicate. A lot of intuition, openness and focus is necessary. It is very intense, requires preparation and intention with assistance of Spirit Guides.

The following is communication, through a *Medium*, with my husband's Spirit from the other side.

Fishing, did he like fishing? I see a dark-haired man - was he dark haired? There are several people coming through - someone who is anxious, or appears excited to speak. I'm seeing a canoe, a small boat. Was there a boat? An island with rocks and trees. I'm seeing a big fountain. Did you travel through Europe? *(This was reference to a big, European-looking fountain, which Steve bought for me a month or so before he died.)*

I'm seeing a little boat, he's showing me - like they hit something. Water, extremely cold, he's showing me a hole, hit something - in front, trying to patch a hole, there's a jerking, it was almost like a whip-lash. Does it make sense to you? It was the cold, panic setting in the heart. He's showing me his heart. Tumbling, flying forward. He's showing me it was like they hit something, hit a *gorder*, it shocked them. He is calling it a *gorder*, it hit and shook them. *(I believe they hit a "water-soaked log", which ripped the motor right off. The boat was submerged with its bow out of the water.)*

I'm seeing a re-enactment: they had heavy gear on - they knew when they hit the water - they're trying to fix it - working really hard to lift it. It flipped; they thought they could fix it. There's a hole. They were trying to patch it. They tried to lift it, get it upright; it was a struggle. They definitely worked on it a long time. Exhausted, they put their heads down to rest a while. At one point, they thought, "We're in big trouble here. Oh my goodness!" They rested too long. A euphoric feeling hit them. It was the cold, they drifted into a very deep peaceful sleep. Chest - heart - the weight - of trying to get the water out of the bow of the boat. His buddy, the skinnier one, left first.

*"It was a state of shock, but you somehow knew that this was going to happen and your intuition of this was a calming. And if you wondered if there was suffering, there was no suffering at all, at all. We just drifted into a very deep peaceful sleep. It sounds kind of, off, but there was a gaping sensation, panic but laughing; we knew our demise. There was panic, but a knowing of our demise."*

*"We chose to go together. This was not an accident. It was our time, that's why it was such of a mystery that it was. It didn't exactly happen the way the truth of how it was going to happen. There was a remembrance, that's why there was such a mystery involved, it should have been more of an accident than it was a mystery. But it didn't happen to the truth of how it was suppose to happen. The brother-in-law fell asleep first, my thoughts drifting quite a bit in that cold. I knew that shock that you were sensing all day, but you knew this was part of a Divine Plan."* He says, *"But you do understand he left the plans early, you kind of had a sense."*

You have seen him in the house walking - he was pleased you were in tune with his presence. *(Yes, I did see him.)* He's mentioning a tall vase with a warped or white flower in it. *(I had a tall vase with a white artificial flower in it, sitting on my fireplace mental. He was trying to give proof that he was indeed my husband communicating and that he knew things about me.)*

He does come and sit on the right side, at the foot of the bed and watch you sleep sometimes at night. He will often sit there and just watch you sleep. He thought maybe you would sometimes feel cramps on your feet. Have you felt his presence? *(Yes, I have.)* Is there is a dog? A white, a special needs or a hunting dog? Did you have a dog? *(My son and his family had just purchased a light coloured Brittney Spaniel dog.)* He talked about being pleased with how I was able to cope, and he was pleased the way everything was handled.

He said, *"When I went hunting, I enjoyed walking through the bush and I felt very peaceful, really enjoying the trees and felt one with nature. Even though it was hunting, it was a peaceful thing for me to do. Do you understand that?"* He's showing me fixing things. Was he a mechanic? I'm seeing a workbench. Was there a workbench? He showed that he loved to fix things on his workbench. He mentioned he was very good at repairing things. *(This was all true!)*

Now, were you planning on going on a trip? *(He mentioned our trip that we were supposed to take to main-land Mexico that winter.)* He said, *"When you were planning that trip, did you know in your heart that it may not happen? It was almost a faking?"(Yes, I went through the motions of tentatively planning the trip, but I seemed to know that it would not happen.)*

Steve mentions that he is aware of what his children and grandchildren are doing. He believes his granddaughter might see him *(his Spirit)* sometimes. He said, *"She was startled a few times, not really understanding what she was seeing."* He is aware of your life and the trip to Cuba and was happy that you did do that. *(I was glad he was still very much a part of our lives.)*

*"I visit you often and didn't really like going anywhere else."* He says, *"In my heart of hearts, I'm enjoying my time back in Spirit, there are no crises here. When you start remembering and knowing; then, it's not so overwhelming to do what you are doing back when you are in Spirit. I am more comfortable in Spirit than I have ever been. You understand what I mean, rather than when I was in body? There are no crises here. I have the ability, I think you know it, to go fishing and do many things, in a different realm, peaceful state, a more state of comfort. There's no worry or friction. There's no need to please anyone, a state of constant contentment."*

He's showing me a particular book, a red book with gold writing, looks like an older book, there's a paper in side, a receipt, nothing significant. *(I did find the book and piece of paper; it was just another confirmation that he knows and is aware of things in my life.)*

*I asked, "Are you aware of what I was learning and was that helping you at all, are you learning through me?"* He is throwing questions back at you, *"Are you aware that now that he is in Spirit that he is learning and studying, to becoming more aware of what is the Truth? For you to be doing what you are doing, you always had that and knew that, and that you can actually feel the presence of a lot of Spirits. With what I'm doing and what you are doing, when you cross over, we'll be on the same plane."* *(He is laughing)* *"I have to catch up to you!"*

The medium mentioned first smelling and tasting a cigar; then, she asked if he smoked when he was on this earth. *(Yes, he did enjoy a cigar now and then.)* He's pretending he is smoking a cigar - trying to be funny. *"I like to enjoy a cigar, but it's way different. You would laugh if you could see what and how I am doing it now."* He keeps mentioning, *"Bob".* *(Bob was a friend, who passed away a few years earlier, I guess he wanted me to know he reconnected with him.)* **He's laughing quite a bit. He thinks it's funny that you are listening to this. He's saying that you don't cry anymore. He is very happy about that. He was not the most affectionate and it really bothered him that he couldn't express himself, and that you'd probably would have appreciated it more. He very much enjoys your laugh!**

**He mentions a book that you are reading - light blue - clouds on it - something about Heaven.** *(I had to try to recall, which book it could be. I asked, "Was it, A Course In Miracles?")* **He said, "No, not that one, but they know about "A Course In Miracles", it's a very, very good book! They know about that."** *(He went back to talk about the book that I was reading.)* **"Something to do with heaven. Maybe some things mentioned in it might be too conflicting for you, but you know to, when you are streaming through your books, how not to believe everything you read. How to weed out things that won't pertain to your growth and happiness."** *(The book he was referring to was, indeed, a book I was reading at that time, the cover was light blue with clouds, "Between Death and Life" by Dolores Cannon. It's past-life regressions and consequent testimonials, revealing many possibilities, some of which could be rather difficult to integrate into one's understanding and acceptance.)*

*"We're learning that the word "belief" is more of a metaphor on how you are filtering things. Life is a mystery, if we were to be told everything and you are intuitive enough, you would stop living in the now and look for too much. You need to stay in the now. That's how I was when I left and the way I left. What better way to leave. There were clouds in the sky, and the clouds and sky opened up, my heart and Soul received and I knew, even though I did not always believe it before, but I understood it. Take a break and enjoy the present time, don't move too far ahead and reach for too much."*

**There's a man who is showing interest in you, he is happy about that one, he is a good match for you. You are in a study group? He just doesn't want it to be too claustrophobic, entwining yourself too much.** *"Give yourself space, listen but step back. Keep doing what you are doing, it's perfect, just be careful not to get too involved with the groups. Know how to filter."* **He wants you to live in the now. That's how he was**

when he was hunting and fishing. *"What better way would I have to leave. Think about that. You know about that. Take a break and enjoy the present time. You know what I mean. I might have, in some ways understood it, but not always believed it."*

He says, *"You would talk, and I would listen; I "would" listen. I didn't always know how, or want to express true feelings, or would jumble words up, and I didn't want to deal with it. I'm not there and it's not any of my business to give you advice, I don't want to give you too much advice, but I'm comfortable enough to give you a little."*

*The medium managed to coax Steve to speak directly through her, these are his words:*

*"Words are often not easy for me to do in Spirit, I am learning to connect with others in my personal skills, to understand that the vast majority of people, here and even over there, are wanting to learn that too. Because when you are on the earth realm, it's a lot different than being in the Spirit, you could call it, realm. There are many cases of people crossing over, the shock of not knowing, not understanding, even grieving for themselves. I never had that. At that moment, I guess I knew, people have different expressions for old Souls, I have been doing this for years.*

*I guess because I haven't evolved as fast as I would have liked, I have been always coming and going, back and forth in quite a few lives. Something I never really paid much attention to, or believed. That's why it was easier for me on that day, in the sense that I knew, my departure was quite simplistic in that way. Because as an older Soul, but maybe not quite as an evolved Soul, I have been spending time over lives doing this, just maybe not learning as much.*

*That's why when you leave the way I left, I knew you could do this. I knew for me it was my time. I was not in a state of shock because I remembered going home, was coming Home. The leaving was maybe more of a tragic way, but we do choose some ways that we can leave, and there are some different graphs you follow. There are often times where you have exit points and your Soul chooses not to. If you want to call your Soul or Spirit, in your physical, chooses not to do that, you could bi-pass that and go with the next. Did you know that? And I bet you did know that I would be learning this again and that those things were happening at the perfect Divine Time.*

*Your presence in this earth is breath-taking, as you have a great circle of friends that respect you and want to draw closer to you. You can keep on doing what you are doing because when you are on earth that is what we do. We come here to express, to learn, to return to love and that's what we are learning here that we are all Love. I will be waiting, I will not be leaving until you complete your cycle because I, without giving you too much, my Guides won't let me pertain to you, as giving you too much of a taste of what I am tasting.*

*When you are finished your cycle you will be at a very evolved level, which we could continue to keep in our group of Souls. Do you follow me? You are going to be okay and you are going to be doing everything you need to be doing at your point. You are following your life path in such a beautiful way that you are able to continue going forth in this world, which will keep other people on your string, your web, on your life.*

*We had a beautiful life and if you want to say, that I have a few words, I had more thoughts in my head than I could express in my words. You have always been more to me than you really knew you were to me, and we had planned this in different scenarios and other ways, so you would not be broken and this was our way of not having you be broken. So you can continue on, go through the doors of the walk, the paths of the life that you have chosen.*

*You need to realize there are very many special people that you will connect to and you'll be able to follow your path, with no more guilt, no regret, or remorse following you. That is not your place in this time to have any of those emotions follow you, do you understand? I am very happy where I am and you should be very happy where you are.*

*Just pay attention to me when I'm around you in the house, around you especially when you are reading, and I will not interfere, as we don't in Spirit and Earth, when you need your private time, or need your other* time. When you need me, I'm just a call away. My love for you will never die, does never die.

You are my perfect angel, perfect in my eyes. If there is a way to say, I miss you, I will always miss you, but I'm not far, I'm so close. We are just in two different realms, two different levels, two different spaces. I'm not as far as you think. It's just if you give the detail we on Earth want, we'll see that and the day will come soon. One day we'll all be able to see that we're just 1 - 2, as Spirit and humans, as we connect, what we do, and go on together.

You go on, keep going, keep your journey alive. We'll be together again.

Love and kisses. Good bye and Good Day!"

# CHAPTER

# 6

# THE RESULT OF NOT FORGIVING

*"The weak can never forgive. Forgiveness
is the attribute of the strong."*

## MAHATMA GANDHI

During my time spent as a volunteer visitor in a hospital/nursing care facility, one of my assignments was a thirty-four-year-old female resident. When I first visited her, she was lying in a fetal position and fed intravenously. Her voice was barely audible and she needed sedation to be turned, or moved because of intense pain. Six months earlier she was a vibrant, healthy, beautiful mother and wife. I read to her and we spent time visiting. Initially, communicating involved a lot of ear straining and lip reading on my part, but visit we did! Her life story quickly revealed why she was so sick.

She was abused by her father, and her mother chose to turn a blind eye. Her attempts to control her world led her into a life of promiscuity, prostitution, and eventually marriage to an abusive, alcoholic man, who promptly left her when she got ill. Her life was filled with self-punishment; she greatly lacked self-love, or love of any kind. Her father, by then, had crossed over. Her mother would visit her and try to spend time with her; however, she often expressed distaste for her and wished she wouldn't visit.

It was not surprising to find her body so full of illness. She was hanging onto private emotions for years, not being able to fully express, or heal from them. Her mind could not deal with so much pain, internalized it and buried it deep, only to have it expressed in the body.

I hoped to help her understand why these things may have happened to her. It would have benefited her greatly if she could forgive people, especially herself, for believing she was responsible in any way. I guided her to imagine her mother's situation, perhaps feeling frightened, powerless, helpless, and paralyzed with fear for an unknown future. She did not have enough inner strength to save her child or herself. Not loving herself caused her to feel she was unworthy of a different life; her will was broken. She resorted to turning a blind eye and remain in complete denial, as an attempt of self-preservation.

So, too, her father, may have been a manifestation of generational behavior. Alone in his private hell, refusing to allow anyone to see his lost and vulnerable inner child; he was emotionally empty, filled with self-hatred, and in extreme psychological pain. His inner and outer life being out of control, drove a need to control others, choosing to control the most vulnerable people in his life. He chose to hurt others in order to distract himself and others from his deep inner pain. Making the problem *out there* not *in him*. Because their religion advocated existence of sin and burning in hell, there was no recourse for him, no escape from hell on earth or anywhere else. To stop his thoughts, he would medicate himself with alcohol, only to find himself totally powerless to choose differently. This led him to repeat his destructive behavior.

Her choices, as well, might have been different if she had been able to express self-love rather than self-hatred. She might have chosen a less destructive path in her own life. She may have inherited her father's control issues and ancestral karma, consequently holding herself responsible for actions of others. But at that time, she behaved, as she believed she needed to. Her motivation was only to kill inner pain, in order to survive. When someone stepped in to guide her, she rejected them and would not accept any help.

It was important for her to forgive herself because she simply had not been aware of an alternative path. Her attempts to be in control and take back her power caused her to be misdirected, inevitably, giving away her power to others; her energy was being drained. Her parents' mental sickness prevented them from being capable of showing love. When one doesn't love oneself, it is extremely difficult to truly love anyone else. It takes a lot of strength and will, to break that cycle.

I let her know that her father's Spirit was around her, and that he regretted the pain he inflicted upon her. He always did and will continue to love her and hoped she could forgive him, more importantly, forgive herself. She would immediately reply, "I hate him, I want to shoot him."

I reminded her that he had already died, she could not hurt him, but her unrelenting hatred of him would persist in hurting herself, instead. These conversations continued for about seven months. Then one day, after asking her, once again, to find it in her heart to forgive, she whispered, "Yes I do."

Perhaps one would question, why was I so relentless in my pursuit? One might think, harm was already done, it is too late to help her physically, or to change anything. One thing I know to be true, holding on to hate requires a lot of energy, energy she did not have to spare. Spending the last of her days in peace and harmony would clearly be more desirable than spending them consumed with hatred and the continued thought induced pain that comes with it. She spent a lot of time thinking.

Most importantly, this may have been her karmic journey. Had she not learned from it, once she crossed over and her mind's knowledge restored, she would realize how she could have chosen differently. She may decide to return to give that lesson another go, a different scenario, but a similar lesson of *forgiveness and self-love*. I was hoping to spare her several lifetimes of pain.

Our script is written. All situations are agreed upon before we are born. These situations, especially ones of extreme stress and pain are opportunities, for us to make choices, whether to be a victim or victor, an opportunity for tremendous Soul growth. Understanding the interplay of others, being able to step out of the drama and see the whole picture without emotional attachments gives one a different perspective and an opportunity for Soul clarity.

## IMPORTANCE OF FORGIVENESS

**"Holding on to anger is like grasping a hot coal with the intention of throwing it at someone else; you are the one who gets burned."[1]**

An inability to forgive others will continue to induce pain within you; you are the one who suffers the permanent harm. The *others* that you believe have hurt you, on the other hand, may not even be aware of any infractions on their part, or they simply may not care. Alienation from others and from society will be the outcome for choosing not to forgive your parents, employers, or other adversaries. You will trap yourself in an unhealthy energy pattern and consequent illness may lead, ironically, to your dependency on those same people for help.

Holding onto resentment may somehow appease our hurt egos; however, we will eventually pay a high price with our emotional, mental and physical health. When it is difficult to forgive oneself or others, there is a refusal of letting go of what one wanted the other person to do or not do, an unconscious desire for self-punishment. The past is passed and cannot be changed, no matter how much we wish it to be different. It's important to ask, "What is it that I'm suppose to learn from this?" Embrace the learning and let go of the emotional pain. When we hang on to past hurts, our concept of what happened lives over and over in our heads. We give it life and are imprisoned by it.

Having read *A Course in Miracles*, I am aware that what we have considered to be forgiveness, has not been real forgiveness. It's important to understand that forgiving others, for their *perceived* hurtful words or behaviors, is far better than harboring a grudge and holding onto pain. Without a doubt, the choice to forgive is a greater challenge than remaining resentful, but this more difficult path will bring immense peace.

Tired of accepting what is and wanting a different life starts a process of loosening chains that keep us prisoners in this cycle of life and death. One's decision to work towards change, triggers a series of countless questions regarding numerous mysteries of who we are and what this world is all about.

This desire for answers starts a succession of events that pave the way to one's truth. Along the way, there is deeper awareness, a realization of how truly lost the human race is. The mind is locked in a pattern of pain and sorrow with no idea how to stop it. Human beings tend to hang on to old hurts and thoughts, refusing to let them go.

## THE MONKEY TRAP

*There is a kind of monkey trap used in Asia. A coconut is hollowed out and attached by a rope to a tree, or stake in the ground. At the bottom of the coconut, a small slit is made and some sweet food is placed inside. The hole on the bottom is just big enough for a monkey to slide his open hand through, but does not allow for a closed fist to pass out of it. The monkey smells food, reaches in with his hand and grabs the sweet food; then, tries to pull it out. Nevertheless, his clenched fist won't pass through the opening. When the hunters come, the monkey becomes frantic, but cannot get away. There is no one keeping that monkey captive, except the force of its own mind's desire. It is a rare monkey that can let go.[2]*

It is our mind's clinging to desires and attachments which keep us trapped. If they are not healed and released, they will shorten our lives by bringing about a demise of the body by sickness and disease. An inability to forgive is poison to the mind, body, and Soul. Scientists have suggested that the evolution of human beings is tied to primates. Our refusal to learn that hanging on to our mind's desires and refusing to let go, even though it would be the death of us, doesn't reflect kindly on the progress of our evolution.

## OUR INNER WORLD IS EXPRESSED
## IN OUR OUTER WORLD

The images and thoughts you hold in your subconscious mind are reflected in your outer world. If you perceive yourself as being poor, you will notice poverty all around you. If you see yourself constantly plagued with illness, you will notice a lot of ill health in your family, or elsewhere in your personal world.

This is true with both negative and positive thoughts and intentions. If you are easy going and generally happy, you will see happiness all around you. If you perceive yourself as unloved, you will see a world devoid of love. If your thoughts are frequently tainted with anger, judgement, bigotry, and prejudice, you will often see it in the world around you. What we see outside of us is really inside of us.

If we are tired of the world we see, we need to look within and change our thoughts and belief systems. Then, we will project the new and improved version of ourselves outward and into the world, which is now also new and improved; it is a reflection of our inner selves. Unfortunately, it took many lifetimes for experiences to be firmly imbedded into the mind and programmed to have certain beliefs and behaviors, it may very well take many more lifetimes to undo all those falsehoods.

A couple of years after my husband's passing, the river running through our community experienced a hundred-year flood. The high water stayed a considerable length of time causing a naturalized park, which runs along the river, to suffer a tremendous amount of damage. The trees and vegetation could not survive the water saturated soil for that duration. The park was devastated. Huge hundred year old Cottonwood, Oak, Bass, Poplar, Maple, and many other trees died, or became susceptible to a fungus, which like a cancer spread through the tree, ultimately killing it. What was not touched by the flood was attacked by an influx of beavers that took down many more trees.

The park looked ugly, filled with death; negative energy permeated the whole area. Other than an occasional squirrel or chipmunk, there weren't many signs of life. I continued to walk through the park, battling mosquitoes and wood-ticks, while focusing on avoiding poison ivy and thistles. I rarely heard a bird, or saw one. What once brought me much happiness now was a sad and depressing place.

Recently, as I walked through the park, I noticed a lot of new undergrowth; ferns seemed to flourish once again along with many young saplings and the bigger trees appeared revived. The branches were thickened with a tremendous amount of healthy, dark green leaves, beautifully canopying pathways. Birds were back, chirping happily, and deer were sighted in various parts of the park.

I was so happy to see not only aliveness again, but was thrilled with the delightfully freeing energy. The dance of light streaming through the leaves seemed to beckon me to stay awhile and enjoy. I commented to my partner how different and wonderful the forest appeared and expressed happiness and gratitude. After reflection, I had that *aha* moment.

At the time of the flood, my outside world was reflective of my mind's flood of emotional turmoil. The expression of death, devastation, and depressiveness was all coming from the inner mayhem in my mind. Several years later, after intense studying, learning, self-analysis, and healing there came a powerful shift in my awareness. I, no longer, viewed the world through dark coloured glasses; my understanding of the world was completely turned upside down and placed firmly upright in a new light. What I was seeing outside of me was the change within me, it was mirroring what was in my mind, which was joy, clarity, truth, and life!

# CHAPTER

## 7

# WHERE IS THE WORLD
# THAT WE SEE?

*"Sit down before a fact like a little child and be prepared to give up every preconceived notion, follow humbly wherever and to whatever abyss nature leads, or you shall learn nothing."*

## D.H. HUXLEY

One day, during a conversation with one of my sisters, I attempted to help her understand why a particular situation didn't actually happen *to* her, it happened *for* her. I said to her, "What you believe to be real, is just an illusion. The truth is that nothing was done to offend, or hurt you because your body and other bodies are not real." She responded, "Well I'm looking at my arm, I'm touching my arm, and it feels pretty real to me!"

This reaction catapulted me into searching for a complete understanding of my statement. It was important for me to express what I had learned, with simplicity and clarity.

I re-read several books, searched the internet for proof, evidence, and explanations to substantiate my statement. I begged my Spirit-Guides to help me, to direct me to simplistic explanations for the possibility of our bodies and this universe to be an illusion. I awoke one night with the words streaming across my mind like writing in the sky:

> ## *"You cannot prove an illusion is an illusion with an illusion."*

I chuckled to myself, somewhat embarrassed by what was now obvious to me. Nevertheless, finding myself and others still within the illusion, I concluded that to reach the *mind* that was entrenched in an illusion, required the use of illusionary tools and explanations.

## OUR EYES DETECT ONLY ENERGY

*"Do not be lonely, the entire universe is inside you!"* [1]

For many centuries, Physicists and Scientists have had multiple theories to explain the mysterious workings of the universe. There are informative discussions amongst prominent Physicists, regarding the fact that nothing is solid and everything in this universe is simply energy, in the article, *Scientists explain the world of Quantum Physics.*[2] Many Scientists and Physicists agree that the universe is made up of energy, constantly vibrating at multiple speeds, bouncing erratically, fluctuating, and moving in waves. Diverse speeds of vibrations cause a vast range of concentrations of pockets of energy, which appear to us in variations of solidity as mass or matter.

Examples of slower vibrating, extremely concentrated, dense pockets of energy could be steel or iron. The faster energy vibrates, the lighter and more translucent it is. Intensely vibrating energies appear as the air we breathe, or the light we see. The highest vibrational field of energy is sometimes referred to as the world of Spirit and is beyond human perception. All vibrating energy is filled with infinite intelligence, and is the field of All That Is.

Animals' senses are more acute than those of humans. You may have witnessed dogs or cats looking off in a direction, and their eyes following something you cannot see. After my husband died, our son noticed that when he entered a room, their family cat would immediately scurry away, as if she saw a ghost. I suspect the energy of Steve's Spirit was with our son at those times; however, he was not able to detect this energy. The cat having this ability became frightened by it; her prompt reaction probably had a lot to do with the fact that she never did like Steve.

Photos taken at our home shortly after Steve's funeral, had circular, transparent, and snowflake-like patterns everywhere. Many different cameras were involved, so it couldn't be dismissed, as dust on the lens of the camera. That was my introduction to *orbs*, Spirit energy of loved ones who have passed. Our deceased loved ones try to comfort us through the initial grieving process. We are not able to see them; however, digital cameras do capture them. They visit us during family gatherings, still enjoying the family parties.

One of the pictures taken at our first Christmas after Steve's passing, clearly revealed his presence. There is a photo of me and my daughter-in-law chatting at the table, while directly across from me, was a large bright orb. Steve, apparently, was enjoying the conversation and perhaps wishing he could join in. This confirmation of his presence was witnessed many times and did, indeed, bring comfort to me.

Another obvious orb was captured in a photo taken while our granddaughter was decorating the Christmas tree. At first glance, what looks like a Christmas ornament on the tree is a big, beautiful orb. Orbs of varied sizes were observed in other photos both in our home and in our son's home. Our loved ones are only a thought away. Orbs are sometimes referred to as *thought-energy*. That's what all bodies are and will continue to be - *thoughts* in the mind manifested into form.

ORBS

Thought Energy - Spiritual Entities

## WHY DO OUR BODIES LOOK AND FEEL REAL?

*"You also believe the body's brain can think. If you but understood the nature of thought, you could but laugh at this insane idea. It is as if you thought you held the match that lights the sun and gives it all its warmth; or that you held the world within your hand, securely bound until you let it go. Yet this is not more foolish than to believe the body's eyes can see; the brain can think."*[3]

What appears to be solid is not solid at all. An article in the *Encyclopedia Britannica*, discusses various unites of energy that are the *fundamental constituents of all matter.*[4] Scientists have broken energy into a world of molecules and atomic particles vibrating violently, orbiting and bouncing off each other. The basic particle of matter, the atom, is composed of a dense, positively charged nucleus. Within the center of the nucleus are subatomic particles, positively charged protons and neutrons containing no charge. Orbiting the nucleus is a cloud of negatively charged electrons, all pulsating and moving erratically at tremendous speeds. Stephen Hawkins once suggested that when you break down the smallest of the smallest particles to its' core, what one simply finds is a vibration of *light*.

The scientific community has concluded that 99.9% of matter is empty space. An article in by *Steve Gagnon*, in *Jefferson Lab - Science Education*, states that the *amount of empty space in an hydrogen atom is 99.999999999996%*.[5] Physicists make multiple comparisons regarding the vastness between planets in the cosmos as being similar to the space between electrons. If the size of an atom is equal to the size of a massive building; then, a ten-cent coin would be the size of a nucleus. There are suggestions that the amount of energy found in a cubic centimeter of space is much greater than all the energy in the total mass of matter that makes up our entire universe. Our universe, which appears so massive and solid, is minuscule compared to all the empty space. The visual universe makes up less than 5% of the mass of the universe.

The conclusion is that the universe and all that is in it, is mostly empty space around which subatomic particles buzz around at tremendous speeds. It is mind boggling to truly fathom the vastness of empty space in all things that are in this universe. Yet our brains cannot compute this to be true. Could it be because our brains don't actually compute anything?

If one takes an intensely powerful microscope and looks at the composition of huge beams supporting a bridge, a chair, or one's arm, one would see mostly empty space. The lower vibrations reduce the vast space within the erratic movements of subatomic particles, causing them to exist in concentrations so immense they *appear* solid. But the truth is, they are mostly empty space.

A simple example of how different vibrations of energy dictate the appearance of solidity, is the observation of a fan. When a fan is on low speed, one can clearly see individual blades, which appear to be solid with spaces between. When a fan is on high speed, it takes on an appearance of a singular blur of transparent energy.

We *believe* we feel softness of the skin on an arm, and when pressure is applied, we even feel bones as well. Nevertheless, this experience is reduced to rhythmic movements of subatomic particles with nothing noticeable or identifiable to our senses. Physicists say that an atom is actually an invisible field of an intense force. A kind of a minuscule twister, through which electrical energy is emitted. Energy and light are being emitted and absorbed by the atoms continually.

Atoms make up everything in this universe including our bodies. Our bodies are concentrations of slow vibrations of energy fields. Energy never dies, it simply changes in intensities of vibrations. Consequently, the mass or objects we perceive eventually change form, as the vibrating rate of energy changes. This ocean of different intensities of vibrating energy and intelligence is what creates the universe we believe we see.

We believe everything we observe: the cosmos, the earth and all within it, including our bodies, are all different. In truth, all are made of the same energy, just composed of multiple variations of vibrations; thus, appearing different. What is in front of our eyes and around our bodies are just pockets of energy behaving differently in a continuance flow.

## WORLD WE SEE IS ONLY IN THE MIND

*"All experiences are preceded by mind, having mind as their master, created by mind."*[6]

The accepted scientific explanation of how our world is perceived by our physical bodies, is that our eyes serve as a lens of a camera. A clear visual example along with an explanation of how the eye works is in an article posted by *Canadian Keratoconus Foundation.*[7] The (light) mass of vibrating energy outside the body, surrounding and encompassing the body and everything in our universe, strikes the optic nerve in the retinal cell of the eye. An electrical signal is sent to the visual cortex, located at the back of the brain, where it is; then, decoded into a three-dimensional, upside-down image, the image of what we believe we see outside our bodies.

This is similar to the way movie images are projected from a movie reel onto a screen. The movie reel is really individual frames of pictures projected out at a high speed, giving an appearance of being uninterrupted by breaks that are between them. Our body's screen is the visual cortex, supposedly at the back of the body's brain. The vibrating energy outside of body is constantly blinking in and out, like a twinkling star, at a speed of millions of times per second.

The truth is that everything flickers in and out of existence millions of times per second. Everything including this world continually and intermittently blinks in and out of existence; this happens so quickly the mind is not aware of it. What we believe we see with our eyes, also flickers in and out with constant interruptions; however, it appears on our inner screen as being a continuous unbroken flow of images. It's like a mirage appearing; then, disappearing quickly. We miss the *blink*; the senses are too slow to pick it up.

Another article in the *Encyclopedia Britannica,* lists a variety of senses that are activated and combined on a daily basis to give us the world we believe we see.[8] All our other senses, hearing, touch, smell, and apparently a total of as many as 17 senses or more, are organized and combined with all other data processed by the movie reel in our minds, creating what we believe we see. All our past memories, programming, thoughts, beliefs, and attitudes are added to the fine tuning and editing of the movie, to create a three-dimensional concept of the world we *think* we see outside of our bodies. Our life's experience is our personal movie.

If we look in a mirror and believe we see our eyes, we are actually viewing the *image* of our eyes in our mind, which we are told is in a brain in our heads. The movie entitled, *Our World*, is playing on a screen inside the head of a body. How is that possible? So, what, exactly, are we seeing with our eyes, outside of our bodies? Our eyes only detect energy that is outside of a body. The eyes and body are also just energy, so according to science, energy is observing energy. It is impossible for us to see anything inside our heads. Where is this image and who is it that is actually witnessing and experiencing it?

Thought is also energy. Imagination, which is formed by thoughts is; therefore, energy as well. Imagination is the creative part of the mind, infinite intelligence.

It may be possible that the mind *is outside of space and time* and encompasses everything in this world, the field of *All That Is*, which is in time and space. Time is created to give an appearance of a succession of events, and space allows creation of holographic images, within the mind. In *Psychology Today*, an article by *Dr. Peter Fenwick, Ph.D.*, a highly regarded neuropsychiatric, *Does Consciousness Exist Outside the Brain*, concluded that indeed consciousness exists independently and outside the brain. That it is part and parcel of the universe such as matter and dark energy or gravity.[9]

The mind is a *device* for receiving communication from two voices, *the ego and Higher Self*. It activates the decisions made and assumes full consciousness of the life and path chosen. The mind is not in the body, its awareness is only in the body. It is outside of time and space and supplies *creative energy- infinite intelligence* for the *imagined world*. It is plausible to conclude; therefore, that within the mind, where creative energy lives, the universe is a creation of the mind's imagination fed by thoughts. All are simply energy.

# CHAPTER
# 8

# WHERE EXACTLY
# IS THE MIND?

*The Creative Mind is outside of Time and Space.*
*A field of infinite intelligence*
*filled with pure consciousness*
*imagining a world within Time and Space.*
*A world that is believed to be real.*

Just recently in a documentary, Scientists were studying anti-matter and matter. They looked at the amount of matter that existed and found that there was an equal amount of anti-matter. They concluded that anti-matter canceled matter. Laughing, the Scientist stated: *"In which case our universe doesn't exist, it is simply nothing."* Apparently, we have been making a big deal out of *nothing*.

Our world, which we believe is real, is just a concept within the mind. The mind is non-corporeal or non-material; non-spatial and non-temporal; it is intangible and invisible. The mind is outside of time and space; it is not in a body, or in this world. The mind surrounds and encompasses all that is part of this universe and beyond.

A personality is really just a composition of various concepts. It is merely a total of memories and conditionings that are projected onto an imagined body within the mind. If the mind's awareness from a body is removed, the body no longer exists, which is what happens when a body dies. The *memory* of the personality and its experience continues to exist in the fractured mind.

The dictionary meaning of concept is: something conceived in the mind, a result of a thought - an idea, invention, or plan. Something that has been thought, or that might be imagined. It is a formulation of an idea, the process of arriving at an abstract idea, belief, or the moment at which such an idea starts to take shape or emerge.

Our life experiences, our bodies and the world we think we see, are simply concepts of the mind. I also believed that my mind was in my brain, in my head and I was a body. Nevertheless, there were times, that I seemed to be observing the scene, and I could hear and see my body. Like watching a scene within a movie in which I was an actor. There apparently was two of me, an observer and the one being observed. It felt like an *out-of-body* experience. Probably because that's exactly what it was. The *I* that *I* really am, never was, nor will ever be in a body. The real I, the mind, has only the *awareness* of being in a body.

## NEAR DEATH EXPERIENCE

When I was in hospital for necessary surgery, I was given too much anesthetic for my body size. An experience that followed left an undeniable and an indelible imprint within my mind.

*I found myself floating above the bed, completely detached from any emotions toward the body lying there. For all I cared, it was completely unimportant, totally meaningless and worthless to me. I could see the nurse beside the bed and intravenous tubes attached to the body.*

*I felt myself slowly moving away, through a mist-like veil into a gaseous essence with delicate wisps of translucent and vaporous-like substance gently melding into one another, effortlessly drifting toward a distinctly illuminated space. I was completely suspended within it as I moved in it, with it, was it and it was me.*

*A heightened state of euphoria, slowly and assuredly, crept through me, as indescribable unconditional Love surrounded me. I was nothing, yet* everything. I was all of that! Love, boundless, endlessness, and eternal! An overwhelming awareness of absolute freedom and peace consumed me.

There was no sense of a body.

I wanted to remain where I was and had no desire, or intention to return. Nevertheless, a voice suddenly got my attention. The nurse called my name, and I was immediately sucked back into the body; within a split second, I was out again and in that wondrous space. Once more, the nurse called my name. Yet again, I returned; then, promptly left. I wanted to scream at her, "Shut-Up!".

The third time she called, I returned into the body with a tremendous thump. Immediately, feeling incredible constraint and a complete loss of freedom. It was as if I was sucked into a block of concrete and bound by chains; I was being imprisoned. I was aware of unbearable pain in every part of the body and having a clear distinct thought, specifically noting, "It is extremely painful to be in a body." Everything hurt, my body was a big mass of pain!

I remained in the body this time. The nurse looked at me and said, "Thank goodness, I had my finger ready on the code blue button." Needless to say, rather than being thankful, I was furious with her. Ever since that day, my mind aches with intense longing to experience that feeling of freedom, peace, and love of what felt to be a natural state of what I really am.

That experience made it clear to me that we were more than our bodies and this world. In fact, somehow, we aren't even attached to it; it is foreign to who we really are. It triggered a forgotten memory within my mind. There are endless debates about the validity of near-death experiences. Questioning how it is possible for a body to travel anywhere. The physical body did not travel anywhere. There is simply *an awareness* of being in a body with a particular name, experiencing a life in an imagined world.

At the time of the near-death experience, the mind removed its' awareness from the body and became aware of travelling into another vibrational realm. It was a simple shifting of awareness, from one thought to another, within the mind. A thought of existing in a slow vibrational state, to a thought of being in a higher vibrating state. Everything we believe we experience is simply in the mind!

# WHAT ARE THOUGHTS?

What is the definition of a *thought*? Scientists and Physicists tell us, *it is waves of a complex pattern of neuron activity*. The Webster Dictionary definition for *thought* is: the power to imagine, an idea, plan, or a conception produced by mental activity; to think, to form or have in the mind, to call to mind, to form a mental picture of. *The thought crossed my mind.*

All thoughts are in the mind, not in any perceived bodies, or anywhere in this universe. The entire universe and all that is within it, is merely a *thought* in the mind. This explanation also applies to the endless thoughts that we believe are in our heads, the thoughts, we think we think. All are within a thought, within the imagination of mind, which is outside of time and space, believing it is experiencing a life through a body. The body is not real, it's only a thought visualized within the mind. The mind's *belief* that it is a body, is a BIG PROBLEM!

So, who or what am I? I am definitely not a body. I am a part of a mind, believing it is a body that is separate from everything and every other body, in a universe believed to be real. The mind is delusional! If you find yourself in this universe and since you are reading this, you are in this same illusionary world; then, you are the other fractured parts of the same sick mind, believing it is separated and different from parts of itself.

The others, you believe you see outside of yourself, those who seem to be completely different and separate, are just *you*. The mind has fractured itself into individual pieces. It is one mind believing it is many. There is no one else out there just me or you, depending on the individual perspective and observations of one's world. We are all part of one mind. So, everything including the part you believe to be your enemy is really you! Fractured parts of itself would still be itself, not *others*. A piece of the same apple.

If you slice an apple, the slices would not become other kinds of fruit, every part is still the same apple. We are fractured pieces of one mind in a world (barrel) full of bruised and battered pieces, all completely confused, delusional, and behaving badly. We are busy blaming each other for our bruises and our messes, dragging ourselves further and deeper into the barrel, not knowing how to get out.

What is ego? The ego is the separated part; the part of the mind that believes it is body in a world. Therefore, we see separateness everywhere.

The life-line of this illusionary world is bodies. To divide is to conquer, control and keep the illusion alive. Time and space are essential to ego's concept of this world. It's important to have an awareness of a past, a present and a future. Space and time works wonders in establishing and affirming separateness. The ego has all tools at hand not only to make this world believable, but also to create a prison for the mind that thinks it is real. We, who believe we are bodies, just like our brother Jesus, are in this world, but we are not of this world.

You are a cosmic mind believing, you are a personal mind. You are actually a multi-personal mind. One mind imagining to be many within a thought. It is starting to sound like the body and this universe could be just a *thought*; a concentration of intelligence within a field of intelligence, filled with potentiality. Pure consciousness flows through the field of intelligence and appears as everything in our world. A field of endless possibilities. All is simply energy!

# ARE EYE GLASSES MAGIC?

*"Thus you believe that you can change what you see by putting little bits of glass before your eyes. This is among the many magical beliefs that come from the conviction you are a body, and the body's eyes can see."* [1]

The body is a concentrated pocket of slow moving energy, nothing solid at all. The body's eyes are surrounded by vibrating energy. The pieces of glass, which are also just vibrating energy, have no effect on the mind. Our physical eyes do not see anything. The world, as we know it, all its sights, colours, and all things of the universe aren't outside of a body, all are only in the mind.

I remember when I received my first pair of glasses. On the trip home, I stared out the car window, fixated and amazed by the fact that the clouds, sky, leaves and blades of grass looked separate and so different from what I was used to seeing. How clearly defined and separate everything appeared to be. In the world I was aware of before I got glasses, everything blurred together, all shapes and colours blended into one another. Everything looked connected and one, without defined borders of separation.

I did not realize that what I was seeing appeared different from the world that everyone else was seeing. In retrospect, I had clearer vision before I got pieces of glass to look through. Glasses caused me to see a world of separation, rather than True Reality. Putting pieces of glass in front of our eyes does nothing to create clear vision, if anything, they only serve to substantiate an optical illusion.

Why is the mind not desiring to see through the illusion of separateness? How does not seeing clearly, serve the mind? It only serves the ego mind by reaffirming and sustaining the illusion. Wrong thinking contributes to a belief in the reality of this world and prevents clear vision in the mind. No pieces of glass can change that, change must be made in the thinking of the mind, which is the cause of the problem. Is there a fear of seeing the truth of its Reality? That certainly would be ego-mind's fear.

There were many other ordinary daily experiences that made me question who and where the *I* really was. One such situation was after the use of my food processor. I took out the blade and placed it in the kitchen sink to wash, promptly cutting my finger on the sharpness of the blade. It felt worse than a really, really, bad paper cut. Several weeks later, I used my food processor again, but before I had a chance to dismantle it, my hand not anywhere near the blade, I felt the same intense pain in my finger. I was completely flabbergasted; I did not cut myself!

Who was experiencing the pain? Where was that thought? The *mind* definitely was not being mindful, fully present, in the moment. Perhaps the ego mind, having been through the same old, same old, so many times, just goes on auto-pilot, making stuff up without synchronizing its senses with a body's actions. The mind is not able to break free of the preconditioned responses and programming.

Another odd situation occurred one day, while I was planning supper. I was preparing a sauce and contemplated frying some onions to add to the sauce. Immediately, upon having that thought, I could smell the onion and my eyes started to tear, as though I was chopping it. The onion was still in the pantry. The body wasn't anywhere near the onion, nor was it peeled, or sliced to emit the smell. It was still only in thought form. Who was having this onion experience?

I had been having an issue with dry eyes for a number of months. One day, while reading and watching television, I became aware of how clearly

I could see. I noticed that my eyes were not bothering me and had not for some time. Almost immediately, my vision blurred and my eyes felt so uncomfortable I needed to put drops in my eyes. The ego part of my mind forgot there was supposed to be a problem, until the right mind became aware there wasn't a problem. *What? No problem?* Well, the ego fixed that in a hurry, the problem was back!

This reminds me of a limerick I committed to memory. It puts into perspective how foolish this illusionary world is:

*"There was a young fellow of Deale who said, "Although pain isn't real, when I sit on a pin and it punctures my skin, I dislike what I think that I feel."*[2]

You may have heard of the *phantom* limb syndrome; the limb is no longer attached to the body. How can the body feel as if it was still there? Is the mind replaying that previously taped scene of the movie where the limb is still attached? Has the mind forgotten that the script of the movie has changed?

The mind creates what it chooses to see and experience through a body. In other words, it sets the stage, backdrops, location, actors, plot, and dialogue for a movie called *Earth World*. What we believe we see and experience is written in our individual scripts, with different scripted experiences from every individual's (actor's) perspective. We (body) just follow the script. All decisions are made in the mind, which is outside of Time and Space. The mind is the cause, the body is the effect.

# CHAPTER

# 9

# EXPERIENCES OF ONENESS

*"You are my voice, my eyes, my feet, my hands through which I save the world. The Self from which I call to you is but your own. To Him we go together. Take your brother's hand, for this is not a way we walk alone. In him I walk with you, and you with me.*

## ACIM [1]

In the above quote, which is from a book called, A *Course in Miracles,* Jesus reminds us that we are all one in the Christ Mind. We must assist each other, *take your brother's hand,* so we could reunite as one. Jesus also reminds us that He is a part of us and by using bodies as a teaching tool, together we will heal the mind and reunite in the True Reality.

Everything is energy, information moving endlessly, constantly transforming, as it flows uninterrupted in a field of infinite possibilities, fed by pure consciousness. Gaps are created in our perception by constant fluctuations of different intensities of energy, moving from greater to lesser and back again. Consequently, connectivity and continuity of the flow of energy *appears* to be broken or non-existent. Our mind is unable to perceive existing oneness in all that is. Everything in our world appears to be separate.

To solidify that belief, the ego mind labels and names everything. All plants, trees, animals, parts of our bodies, people, cities, countries, nations, mountains, lakes, oceans, and even clouds are named. It is important to name everything. Names create boundaries, they suggest and affirm separation, me and you, they and us. We label things as possessions, my thoughts, my feelings, my experiences, my body. Who is the *my* or the *me*? The *me* appears to be separate and alone. Nevertheless, the *me* is never alone. Everywhere and all around me are countless other *mes* trying to take center stage, always having one's own best interest at the forefront.

Our insistence that everything is separate, our refusal to see our oneness and take responsibility for others, is the cause of our greatest grief. The ego mind encourages society to nurture and sustain separateness in individuals and groups by celebrating differences. Numerous parades and award celebrations bring attention to a diversity of life styles, sexuality, cultures, nationalities, occupations, the rich and famous, royals, and many others. This process serves to set apart and further alienate society. Making specific groups or individuals more unique, special, worthy, and desirable affirms separation. Everyone else is different from, less-than, not good enough, losers, and not part of the elite, the special ones.

Unfortunately, drawing awareness specifically to a multitude of differences encourages further fragmentation of the totality of a united experience within the concept of the mind. Ideally, movement should be towards sameness of valued contribution to connectedness, wholeness and oneness of all.

All bodies bleed, get sick, suffer pain, know fear, feel guilt, want happiness, desire love, grieve, and die. No matter what classes or status, all humans still experience the same emotions. Our lives depend on others; without others, this world would be meaningless. One experience is not more valuable than any other, and should not be framed as though it is. We are all connected. Our *healed Mind* is capable of expressing it all, there are no limitations. All parts of the whole are still the same as the whole.

Many opportunities are presented in one's life to notice oneness in everything around us such as being fully present, while viewing a beautiful lake, mountain scene, or an unfathomable wonder, which takes one's breath away. It's being in the moment, completely absorbed in the now, when time appears to stand still. It is at that moment, Right-mindedness, Higher Self, Jesus, or Holy Spirit is able to bring the mind's full awareness to total connectedness and oneness of all that is, a perpetual natural way of being, our True Reality.

Please note: Right-mindedness, Higher Self, Jesus, or Holy Spirit are one and the same; choose whichever one you are most comfortable with.

## OUT OF BODY EXPERIENCES

During my search for truth, I journeyed on several different roads to investigate many possibilities. One of which was an interest in *out of body travel*. *Robert Monroe* experienced travelling out of body, leaving his body while fully conscious. In his book, *Journeys Out of the body*, he shares his many travels. He founded the *Monroe Institute*, a non-profit organization, researching out-of-body possibilities. My interest was further engaged by *Paul Elder's* book, *Eyes of an Angel*, in which he detailed his experiences with this phenomenon.

I listened to hemi-sync music and concentrated on having an out of body experience. One evening, I was aware of floating near the ceiling of my bedroom, moving effortlessly through the wall and observing my living room from the level of the ceiling light fixture. I felt removed from my body, but somehow still had a semblance of an awareness of a body. I was completely conscious of being above the room, having a bird's eye view of the room. I got all excited and before I knew it, I was back in my body. I continued to do the exercises and was determined to have another experience, perhaps relax enough to go beyond my living room.

When I had an opportunity to take part in a *Guidelines Retreat*, a *Monroe Institute Gateway Voyage program* at a resort on the Island of Victoria, I made a decision to go. Typical of the Guidelines Program, we spent a couple of sessions every morning and afternoon, in our rooms with earphones on, listening to hemi sync music and guided meditation. In between each session, we would get together in a conference room for debriefing and sharing. A number of participants shared interesting interactions with Spirit Guides, while travelling out of body.

Nevertheless, for me, the week was mostly uneventful, or at least nothing more than usual experiences I would have during meditation. Before one of the meditations, I said to my Higher Self, "Okay, Self, take me on the ride of my life." Hoping to have a different experience. Well, I guess I did because there was an adorable puppy licking my face (not literally, of course, but an experience in my mind). It was not exactly what I hoped for, but I accepted it gracefully.

The next day began with a short film, beautifully composed with captivating landscapes, along with a narrative of divinely inspired words, transporting us to a familiar place where a part of us always yearns to be. This blissful state stirred a memory tucked deep in my heart. I was profoundly moved and completely oblivious to a flow of tears running down my face. After the film, much to my relief, we were told to go outside and walk, or spend time alone, silently, until being summoned for the next meditation session.

As I walked, still caught in an emotional space of homesickness, I stepped into a wooded area and just stood there admiring massive, ancient trees. All of a sudden, the three-dimensional things I was observing were magnified many times. I was drawn to patterns, roughness, smoothness, multiple layers, countless shades of color, and deep lines of time embedded in the structured surfaces of the trees. There was an acute awareness of a pulse, a heartbeat, as I listened intently in anticipation of hearing great wisdom previously locked away.

My attention was drawn to moss inching its way up the trunk of the tree; delicate fingers weaving patterns and fondly caressing the open wounds of time. Leaves, at first glance, seemed uniquely diverse, appeared oddly similar revealing a supple melding of colors, while reaching and blending with the seamlessness of oneness beyond.

Blades of grass, revealed a variety of shades and intensities of colours, along with a multitude of identical veins, notches, and lobes, lovingly embraced by the tree's network of roots. All binding and intertwining with fragments of stones imbedded in soil, purely an augmentation of one another, becoming united and one, while joining in union with Mother-Earth.

The clouds looked as though within reach, billowy, soft and eloquent, affectionately inviting me to play with them. Even the sky was in sync with this composed melody. Branches reaching, gently stroking, graciously waving, as they harmoniously conducted the energetic and magical flow of continuance.

Everything that was around me was a extension of the same grand symphony; beauty and wonder mesmerized me. It was as though I was breathing it, living it, and was it. Then, I heard a voice very clearly, and at the same time I heard it, I also felt that I was the one who was speaking. *"You are my eyes, my ears, my voice."* Who was I?

Still surrounded by an uninterrupted flow, I was drawn to a large spider web and proceeded to examined it through the eyes of a child, completely enthralled. Elaborately detailed, fragile, and silky, lace-like designs created with artistic and mathematical precision into a work of art and function.

Following its outline, my attention was drawn to a huge spider; I studied it with a microscopic sight in observing minute details. The beauty and intricacy of its body, its remarkable constructs of numerous appendages performing flawlessly in unison. Shades, colors, textures, compositions, and functionality of its makeup caused me to be absolutely in awe of the intelligence that created it. As I moved away, I heard clearly in my mind, *"You have been looking out there, outside of you, but it's all within you. YOU are the ride. Simply be aware, Simply Be."*

Suddenly, I felt embarrassed and ashamed like a child engaged at play, unaware a parent was watching. A child fully engrossed in a pretend game of life, acting out parts, and talking imaginary conversations. I had forgotten who I really was, my True Identity. I was swept up into a virtual reality game, really wanting to play the part. There was an intense feeling of unconditional love and acceptance; that it was *okay.* I was reminded that I, Jeanette, was a made-up character, who's life journey is the *trip.* Everything in this universe is connected and not separate; all within one thought in the mind.

## CONNECTING WITH DOLPHINS

**"Whoever has parted from his source longs to return to that state of union."** [2]

Another very memorable experience was in the Sea of Cortez, Baja of California, Mexico. Steve and I were fortunate to be able to experience travelling with our 5th wheel trailer into Mexico. One of the places we enjoyed, was camping at a beach in the quiet bay of La Conception, on the Sea of Cortez. The water in that bay had a reputation of being as still as glass, most nights and early mornings. It was a popular bay for kayaking.

One winter we loaded our sea kayaks on top of our truck and 5th wheel trailer and off we went. I have always been drawn to water, but also held a great deal of respect for its power. Before this adventure, we took lessons in kayaking, wanting to be safe, to know how to rescue one another if something unforeseeable happened. Steve was probably more than double my size, so it was imperative that I was able to rescue him and/or myself, if need be.

Every morning, we donned our life-jackets, and I put on my dorky looking hat. We enjoyed exploring the many islands and shorelines, making a point of sticking close to land; I did not feel comfortable otherwise. Steve was a naturally strong man. As we paddled, he would take one sweep of the paddle, while I would have to take ten in order to keep up to him. The stillness of the moment was constantly interrupted by me yelling at him, "Wait for me!"

One morning, while we were out in our kayaks exploring, we spotted a pod of dolphins. We cautiously moved closer toward them. Before I knew it I was in the middle of the pod, moving completely in harmony and in sync with them, totally drawn into their energy, their psyche, and utterly hypnotized by their melodic sounds. Words fail to describe the exhilaration of the moment, the ecstatic high, a sense of floating and being suspended between two realities. I was entirely oblivious to my body, or anything else.

The protection that encompassed me and unconditional love that embraced me was tangible. Time, literally, stood still! Nothing was important, except what was at that moment. No-thing existed other than total union with the dolphins, one body, one Spirit. This was where I belonged and certainly where I wanted to stay.

Nevertheless, something jarred me out of this trance-induced state and was very quickly becoming an irritant. As much as I tried not to notice it, it finally reached a point where it was downright aggravating and impossible to ignore. In order to decipher what it was, I needed to slow down and really strained to listen.

It was a voice way in the distance, which I recognized to be Steve's voice, faintly saying something that sounded like, "Jeanette what are you doing? Can't you see they are taking you further into the ocean?" I looked around me and saw only a large expense of water, with no hint of land. Then, I saw the dolphins pulling away; my heart sank. "What to do? What to do? Need to choose! Husband or dolphins? Husband or dolphins?"

By then, I realized it would be difficult to catch up to the dolphins; suddenly, the powerful human emotion took hold of me - *fear*. Cautiously, I manoeuvred the kayak through turbulent water, left by the wake created by the dolphins, and reluctantly paddled back towards my husband. I still couldn't quite hear him, but I could see that (as he used to say to me), his mouth was *going like a duck's ass*. Yeah, I know, he was a keeper!

When I finally reached him, he had calmed down somewhat and said to me, "What on earth got into you? I tried to keep up, but I couldn't!" We paddled in complete silence back to our campsite, trying to compute what had just happened.

Reflecting upon my late husband's words, "What got into you?", I was aware that nothing had gotten into me, it was already in me. I had tapped into an energy field, a force, a knowing already within my mind and connected with *All that is*. We are all *It*, all connected, always one with *It*. There is within us all, an awareness gently guiding us toward a desire to be united with wholeness and oneness. The Aquarian Age encourages a global movement toward oneness, as we awaken to sounds of Love, always there, waiting patiently within each and every one of us. Can you hear it?

# CHAPTER

# 10

# IS THIS THE ONLY UNIVERSE?

*"In a gentle way you can shake the world."*

## MAHATMA GANDHI

In every atom, there are worlds within worlds. Within our physical bodies, and everything else that exists in this universe, are atoms within which are mini universes. In an article *Parallel Universes - Alternative Universes Explained,* Scientists and Physicists have come to numerous conclusions and proposed various theories regarding our universe.[1] One such theory is that we are living in a matrix, a computer simulated reality.

At every crossroad in our lives, with every major decision we make, there is a parallel universe within which we exist, living the experience of an alternative decision. With that awareness in mind, it is easy to understand that there may be infinite number of universes. We are in a holographic universe within which there are endless number of universes with equally endless possibilities; many dimensions vibrating at various speeds within the same space as our dimension. Similarly, different radio stations can occupy the same space at the same time because they operate at different frequencies. To tune into another station, simply adjust the dial to connect with a multitude of frequencies. These frequencies exist at the same time in the same space.

A hologram is an illusion of appearances of objects where there are none. In an article, *The take: Big ideas Explained in under five minutes*, by *Matthew Headrick*, an assistant professor in physics at Brandeis University explains the holographic principle and how it is possible for the universe to be a hologram.[2] A mirror is a rudimentary example of how 3-dimensional images can be seen where they are not. I recall a situation when I was shopping at a shoe store, I was enjoying all the shoes, picking them up and admiring them. I reached out to pick up a pair that caught my eye and proceeded to smack my hand into a mirror. This caused quite the racket and attracted the attention of all the other customers. I quickly existed the store with a bruised hand and somewhat bruised ego.

Apparently, there was a huge mirrored wall behind the table of shoes, intending to create an illusion of more space and more product. The shoes appeared 3-dimensional and very real to me, but they were only an illusion created on the solid flat silvering surface of the mirror. There was simply an appearance of depth and space, which is exactly the case with everything in our universe. Time and space are illusions.

## CONVERSATIONS WITH STEVE'S SPIRIT

During one of many conversations I had with the Spirit of my deceased husband, he said he was not far away from me. I persisted in knowing, *"Exactly how far away?"* He finally replied, *"I'm just a thought away, I'm right beside you."* *"Yes, but how far?"*, I asked. *"Inches away"*, he responded. A thought away is certainly not far at all. Could this be because everything in this world is in the same mind? All the thoughts of everything that existed in the past, along with all thoughts of potentially infinite future possibilities, exist today, at the same time, in the same mind. No different from your day to day thoughts that you believe are in your head. All you have to do is *think* of someone and there they are, in the mind. Your thoughts, body, the world and cosmos are all in the one mind.

# LUCID DREAM

I struggled to fully understand how parallel universes were possible and could occupy the same space at the same time. I asked my Guides to help me. That answer came to me within a lucid dream.

*I was observing a busy city-street scene, witnessing a variety of backgrounds in various degrees of transparency - superimposed upon one another as well as what appeared to be numerous layers of people. Human beings of different concentrations of solidity and transparency scurrying about in multiple directions. They were occupying the same space, passing through one another and were oblivious to each other. I watched, confused at first; then, I received clarity. It was at that point that I became aware of a presence beside me, and through "thought transfer", I was asked "Do you see them?" I replied "Yes, I see them."*

It was clear to me how it was possible to have an infinite number of universes vibrating at different frequencies, occupying the same space at the same time and be unaware of each other. I often wondered if during occasions when clear out of the blue, my body would momentarily shudder, as though feeling a chill, whether someone just walked through me. A higher vibrational energy flows through a lower vibrational body of energy.

# MEDIUMISTIC ABILITIES

Since all is in one space, it is a matter of dialing into that frequency, like a radio. All information is accessible, the past, present and future. I was able to serve as a medium, delivering messages from deceased loved ones to those still here in this dimension because it was all within one mind. It was an ability to simply go to an imagined place in the mind and clearly see physical images, observe the characteristics, mannerisms, personalities, attire, occupation, and other crucial information. I had no prior knowledge of any of that information. All communications appeared to be by *thought transfer*, accessing a thought within one space.

During Time-line regression, this same ability to retrieve information is also at play. It's just a matter of accessing a different vibrational dimension within the same space. All the information of past lives is available because it exists at the same time, same space, and in the same mind. Information regarding future lives is also available. Understandably, those are more difficult to access. We would not be able to continue with our lives if we knew of our possible future, which depending on our choices exists in infinite possibilities. It is the same reason we come into this world with a veil of forgetfulness drawn over any memory of past lives. Forgetfulness is necessary in order to focus on learning through our present life's experiences.

## TRAVEL TO A DIFFERENT DIMENSION

Scientist and futuristic inventors have been dabbling with technology determined to invent a time travel machine. The intention would be to travel through a worm hole to parallel universes. They appear to be focusing on transporting a human body through this worm hole. It's not an actual physical body, which is *believed* to be solid and real, that could be transported.

It would be the *awareness of a body* that could travel through worm holes (gaps) within the structure of fluctuating energy that encompasses *thought universes*. It's the mind's *awareness* of being a body that is transported to another dimension, not a body that we believe is real, but an illusionary body. Time travel is possible now and happens within the mind. I believe that I had such an experience.

*One morning, while lying in bed, meditating, I focused on a tiny black spot in my mind's eye. Before I realized what was happening, I had a **sensation** of travelling at indescribable and unperceivable speeds. Ultimately, finding myself still travelling; however, now at a greatly reduced speed, gently floating through the air, through what appeared to be a typical neighborhood. I was aware of trees, grass, roads, and homes, as well as having an ability to see though the walls of buildings, observing people in their everyday lives.*

*At one of the houses, my attention was drawn to a particular room by adorable cooing sounds of a baby and a mother's loving response. I paused there momentarily to linger in the joy of that experience when the dark haired women turned and looked at me, our eyes met and I just knew, I was her, she was me, in another life experience.*

*Totally caught off guard, I lost elevation immediately. I felt **my phantom body** grazing the ground, actually **feeling** the grass and small stones on what would have been the back of my body, even though there wasn't an actual body, just an assumption of a **body**. I absolutely knew that **my body** was still in the bed in the house, which I knew as my home.*

*I was completely confused and bewildered. How is it possible, for me to have had those sensations that felt so **real**? I realized that the real me was very much alive, not confined to, or needing to identify with a particular physical body. That all the emotions and seemingly physical sensations were not experienced in the body, they were experienced **only** in the mind. I was the mind experiencing life through a body. I started to panic and could not get off the ground, try as I might to lift off. I continued to skim the ground. Frantically, I called out to my Spirit-Guides, "Please help me". **Immediately**; I found myself back in the body lying on the bed in my home.*

How was all this possible? This was not a night-time dream, I was awake and in the process of beginning to meditate. Did I travel through a worm-hole or a black hole into a parallel universe? If I had not activated and engaged the powerful emotional reaction, *fear*, I would have continued with that experience. Is it *fear* that keeps us *tied* to this world? This experience confirmed what I was already starting to believe was true; that all the *body's senses* and *experiences* of this universe are *only* in the *mind*.

The body is not real, bodies are only puppets, pawns in a virtual reality game. The mind is the producer of the experience, as well as the one having it. The mind is able to superimpose its awareness completely into a body, like an actor in a movie and experience life through that imagined *thought body*.

## How do Senses Work?

*"The mind's capacity is limitless, and it's manifestations are inexhaustible. Seeing forms with your eyes, hearing sounds*

*with your ears, smelling odors with your nose, tasting flavors with your tongue, every movement or state is all your mind."[3]*

I recently watched a *Nature of Things Documentary* regarding many experiments that were conducted to establish how our senses work.[4]

The first experiment was to establish whether seeing was believing. A subject watched, as an illusionist performed a trick involving a ball. At one point, the ball appeared to be tossed up in the air, the subject was sure it disappeared. The illusionist only pretended to toss it up, it was still in his hand. There is a ten second delay between the *thought* and the body's action. One cannot believe what one thinks one sees; eyes failed the test.

Another experiment was to determine if what the eyes saw had any effect on the taste senses. There were samples of juice for testers, one included a drink colored dark purple. The testers said the juice was mulberry or black berry. Another sample was coloured orange, the testers all stated the juice was orange juice, when in fact all the samples were apple juice. Sight influenced taste.

The next test was to determine if hearing interfered with taste. A subject was placed in a booth with head phones on. Three bowls of chips were tested for freshness. The ear phones were fed sounds by a neuroscientist, outside the booth, manipulating what the tester was hearing. The subject listened to high frequency sounds reflecting varied degrees of crispness. The subject gave all three samples of chips different degrees of perceived crispiness. All chips were from the same bag. One cannot believe what one tastes is real; taste and hearing failed the test.

Odors were fed through a mask while names of odors were flashed on a screen. When the words *fresh flower* were combined with the odor of almond extract, a pleasant rating was given. When the odor of almond extract was combined with the words *cheap perfume*, an unpleasant rating was given. The smell sense failed the test.

The next experiment involved seeing along with feeling. A subject's arm was obscured by a curtain. She viewed a (rubber) arm being touched, fully believing that it was her own; at the same time, as her hidden arm was being touched. Convinced that the rubber arm was actually her real arm, she screamed when it was stabbed with a fork. The feel sense failed the test.

The last test, involved watching a film of crawling ants. Does what people see, cause their skin to react? Did the skin rely on sight and suggestion to respond rather than touch? The subjects reacted to the film by scratching their bodies. The feel sense failed the test.

The neuroscientist concluded that multiple senses were at play, relaying information to the brain (the mind). The total relationship of all senses work together to create a specific experience, which the mind's internal model of conditioning is programmed to experience. Our senses integrate to create the perception of our reality.

The conclusion was that the magic happens in the mind, that's where our understanding of the world comes from. What we think we perceive through our senses is not true. Our senses trick us into believing we are having a specific kind of an experience, which serves the mind. Previous to rebirth in a body, patterns of desired experiences are programmed within the mind, including all intended sense experiences.

## HOW DO EXPERIENCES IN A
## BODY SERVE THE MIND?

*"Take someone who doesn't keep score, who's not looking to be richer, or afraid of losing, who has not the slightest interest ever in his own personality. He' s free."*[5]

Each individual mind is drawn to a particular experience to either activate healing of the mind, or simply to give continuous life to *wrong minded* thinking. The mind could choose either with ego, wrong-mindedness, or Higher Self. Recently a sort of an experiment created by *Payless Shoes, in Santa Monica, California,* should assist with understanding some of the workings of the mind.[6]

A former Armani store was taken over by the shoe retailer and renamed *Palessi.* They stocked it with *Payless* merchandise; then, invited fashion influencers to attend a strategic opening. Shoes normally priced $20 - $30 were sold for between $200 and $600. Many of the purchasers noted how the products reflected *sophistication* and praised the *high quality* of the material and craftsmanship. Over $3000 worth of merchandise was sold during the first few hours.

The preconditioned concepts and beliefs associated with value dictated what these shopper believed they saw. What their minds were programmed to see, think, and believe created the world they were to experience. Perhaps a sophisticated name denotes higher standards and values, price could probably indicate higher qualities, all these factors would be part of the programmed script.

So how would these beliefs serve the mind? Perhaps it is essential to belong to a particular group, one that symbolizes success that is driving the mind to search for experiences, which would sustain that facade in their lives. These experiences nurture thoughts of being better, more important, more worthy than those who cannot afford that life style. Wearing these masks could serve to deny and depress feelings of inadequacy and a lack of self-worth. This is an egotistic fulfillment in setting apart, separating, and setting boundaries firmly in place.

What about those who observed people coming out of a shop called, *Palessi*, with fancy bags of purchases? The passer-bys may place those customers on a level above them, an unreachable pedestal of importance and worthiness. Which filters influence their observations, knowing full well that store would be off limits to them? Those that envied them would be contributing to the illusion of their specialness, at the same time sustaining their own beliefs of inferiority. Such thoughts would serve their wrong mindedness by feeding their own belief systems of being losers, less than, not worthy.

Both the rich and poor have sick minds in need of healing. Materialistic worth is an illusion created to distract from one's True Realty, which increasingly becomes impossible to recognize.

It is interesting that this news-clip was not on the news for long. It is important for the ego mind to remove any examples of how ego serves to mislead and deceive the mind into believing falsehoods. The mind has been tricked into believing something is real when it is only an illusion. Sound familiar?

Imagine if someone slaps a fancy name with a price tag to match on a wine bottle and promotes it as a wine that only the rich could possibly afford. It is quite possible that the wine inside may be the cheapest grade or homemade. The perception, that it is expensive, somehow better, and more valuable causes the mind to believe it to be true.

The taste experience is *only* in the mind. It's a belief in the mind that creates the ultimate necessary taste. The programmed accumulated senses will deliver a desired experience of taste to the mind, which would reinforce the feeling of specialness and certainly justify the price. The ego mind requires a particular wrong mindedness thinking to be fed and sustained. But there too, one's True Reality becomes hidden in the unconscious mind, which is obscured by the ego's projected desired image of oneself. Once again, being in denial of the True Self, sustains a belief of lack of self-worth and fuels a desire to be important and special. This serves not only to fool others, but most importantly continue to fool oneself.

Years ago, at a New Year's Eve party, one of the guests brought, what we were told, was a very expensive bottle of champagne. Granted I am not a connoisseur of liquor of any kind; however, I didn't expect the reaction I had when I had my first sip. I expected it to taste amazing; my experience was the opposite.

Perhaps I was the only mind that did not experience the appropriate taste reflective of its monetary value. What one experienced, depended on what the mind needed to experience at that moment. So why did I not choose to be truthful? Was it my mind's need to belong, to feel special, and be a part of this group that caused me to go along with the group facade?

What sickness in my mind was that thought system feeding? Unworthiness, undesired, unloved, unwanted? Maybe that is a problem that ties us to this world. Being afraid of speaking the truth. Was my mind's need to be liked and accepted worth more than speaking the truth?

*This reminds me of a childhood story about an Emperor who apparently received new robes. In order to show off his new robes to his noble subjects, he paraded down a stretch of his kingdom, while his faithful followers and servants lined the street. All humbly bowing, cheering, and praising the beauty of the robes. A child was watching the procession and was completely confused with all the fuss. Finally, he spoke up and said, "But the Emperor has no robes, he is naked".*

Only a child had the clarity of sight and the strength of innocence to speak the truth. The others were obediently going along with the deceit, afraid to step into truth that indeed, the emperor had no robes on at all. *Everyone was tricked by fear, into believing the illusion was real.*

What is important to understand is that it is not about what is in the bottle, whether it's wine or just coloured water. It's not about the price of the wine, the quality, or the price of the shoes. This experience is not in the body, nor in the world. The reality of the existence of any of those things is only in the mind, which gives it form by imagining a thought.

The mind projects a specific intended experience onto a body; then, it becomes aware of the precise perception of reality it needs for that experience. The final experience is created by the filters of the ego mind's belief system.

A life may have been requested, which requires experiencing superiority with the intention of discovering the error of that thought system. If this lesson is not learned in this lifetime, upon rebirth, one may choose a life of a pauper or a homeless person. The lesson the mind may learn is that it is better to experience life from a place of love and oneness, rather than one of superiority and separation.

The world we individually experience, is exactly and perfectly created to assist with the Soul's desired intended spiritual growth during this lifetime. An emotionally driven experience is likely to be more quickly and permanently imbedded in the mind; thus, facilitating a change in the mind's internal program.

Life lessons expressed and experienced are consequently ingrained in our minds much more permanently than intellectual understandings. Every experience in this world leaves an emotional energy imprint within the mind. These emotional imprints are the filters though which we view our world and are the drivers of all beliefs and decisions.

## METAPHORS EXPLAINING LIFE EXPERIENCES

There are many metaphors that can be used to explain this life experience. One metaphor is that life was like a *video game*. It entails a goal, a desired result, or destiny. This is also the purpose of one's life in this world. The bodies are pawns in a three dimensional and demented game directed by some outside force. Someone else makes choices and decisions for the moves that are to be made. There is always a winner and a loser. Sound familiar? Our bodies have no control, or power in decision making. Who is the decision maker? Who makes the choices and influences those decisions? Bodies don't make any choices. Their actions are projected onto them.

Some have referenced to life in this world, as being a *computer program* within which all actions, every detail, and conclusions are written into the program. The programmer establishes the story line. Like pawns or puppets, the body just follows the program. There are many opportunities to rewrite the program, if necessary, for a different outcome. Who is the programmer?

As children we would often have *pretend* play. Little girls would play with their Barbie dolls and boys with their action figures. The child would direct the scenes, engaging the dialogue and actions. The action figures or dolls were not doing any thinking, talking, or decision making. The child, the creator of this pretend story, was the producer, actor, perceiver, and the one having the experience. This is no different than what we believe is our real life. The bodies are not the thinkers; the bodies are only the *pretend action figures*. So, who is the thinker, director, observer and having the experience of the *play* or *story* that is called real life?

This universe could be referred to as a *movie*. The protagonist of the movie has the leading role, as the story unfolds the plot includes interactions with other actors, the people in our lives. We follow the script and act out our parts. If any of those factors are changed in the present moment, the script also changes. All these factors play a big role in our individualized movies.

Perhaps a *comic book visualization* would help us understand more clearly how our world could be a *thought* within a mind. Imagine a comic book, in which one of the characters has a thought; the thought within the mind, takes shape of a balloon with an arrow pointing to the character's head. Within the balloon, is a visualized thought, which encompasses other people having imagined conversations, interactions, and actions. We are the characters within a thought, acting out a scene within the imagined thought. The mind (the comic book character) is the creator of the thought.

The creator is the mind, mistakenly believing it has separated parts of itself from the rest of the mind, creating its own world, movie, video game, or dream, within which it assumes the life of all other characters. It is up to the creator of this thought to change the scene, to choose differently, to create a different script. The scripts, like the computer programs, have many opportunities to be rewritten. There are infinite possible scripts to future experiences in the movie of one's life. It's a sequel to a movie involving generations of lives. Who is the writer, director, actor, and the one having the experience? It is the one Mind.

# CHAPTER

# 11

# ARE DREAMS REAL?

*"What is seen in dreams seems to be very real. Yet The Bible says that a deep sleep fell upon Adam, and nowhere is there reference to his waking up. The world has not yet experienced any comprehensive reawakening or rebirth."*

## ACIM [1]

References to a dream metaphor are made many times as simplified explanations of our lives. This thought system is expressed in the Bible and in many books by renown Philosophers, Scholars, and Spiritualists. It seems that in the Bible, Adam (fractured mind) has been in a deep sleep. Awakening from this sleep is a very slow and painful process because the dream appears to be so real and often frightening.

I had been struggling to understand the concept of this life being a dream. In our night-time dreams, everything within the dream is a part of and one with the dreamer of that dream. There are no invasions by other people into the mind having the dream. They are all part of the one mind, the dreamer, represented by different looking bodies, but they are still part of the dreamer of the dream. Life is a series of day-time dreams and night-time dreams, both are created by one dreamer dreaming of multiple versions of the self.

*"All we see and seen is but a dream within a dream........a hologram within a hologram."*[2]

This fact would also give validity to a truth that we are not separate from other people, or from anything within our universe. It is not possible to be separate from anything that exists only within one mind. Nothing in this universe is separate; we are one, experiencing that we are many.

It was important for me to not only fully understand, but to feel the truth of that statement. Once again, I asked my Guides to help me understand how my life, which seems so real, could be just a dream.

## THE NIGHT-TIME DREAM - DAYTIME DREAM

*One night as I was fast asleep, I found myself to be very much in the midst of a developing nightmare. As the scene unfolded, I was trapped in a hospital bed and in the process of being attacked by a man wearing a doctor's white coat. I could not speak and was unable to call for help. I tried to scream, but was only uttering weird noises. At the same time, I was awakened by those noises.*

*Suddenly, I found myself separate from both the body and the dream, being aware of my sleeping body and my dream, and at the same time I was both. I was observing the unfolding scene in which the body was panicking and completely terrified, as it was struggling to activate the call-button. I felt the full paralyzing terror of this experience.* I was the observer and the one being observed.

*Through thought-transfer, the attacker told me not to bother trying to get the call button to work because he would just say it was pressed accidently and everything was alright. As the observer, I was also viewing that scene as though I were watching a movie, unattached, and unaffected.*

*Suddenly, the sleeping me woke up, sweating profusely, heart racing, and feeling the horror and panic of that moment.* I was so relieved to find myself safe in my bed and in my home. While trying to recover from this emotional trauma, I remember saying to myself *"Wow, that was so real!"* followed by a voice that said, *"Yes, it did seem real, didn't it, but it was only a dream!"*

*"Only after the deep sleep fell upon Adam could he experience nightmares. If a light is suddenly turned on while someone is dreaming a fearful dream, he may initially interpret the light itself as part of his dream and be afraid of it. However, when he awakens, the light is correctly perceived as the release from the dream, which is then no longer accorded reality. This release does not depend on illusions. The knowledge that illuminates not only sets you free, but also show you clearly that you are free."* [3]

What we believe to be real, all of life's pain, fear and discord, is not really done to us at all. The daytime dream is created by ego or our conscious mind, in order to keep us entangled within the illusion. The night time dream is created by our unconscious mind, with the intention of bring to the forefront, an awareness of wrong minded thinking. The night dreams are usually symbolic messages, sometimes in the form of metaphors, needing contemplation and interpretation. Bringing about the question, "What am I suppose to learn from this?" All this with an intention of healing the cause of a particular mental disharmony within the life experience.

Our day dreams are no different than our night dreams. We just move from one dream to another; neither are real. Both are created and observed within a *sleeping mind* believing it is real. The movie, *Inception*, gives us a glimpse of how caught-up we can be in this insane dream world and how difficult it can be to escape it. The ego had a thought and planted an idea in our mind which changed our reality. The True Reality was once known; however, a decision was made to forget. Our lives are composed of moving from one dream to another; we are lost in a foreign world. Nothing we do within the dream is real. We need to forgive ourselves and our projected-selves because nothing happened within an illusion. No-one is guilty of anything.

It's not easy to wake up from this dream. It is necessary to be gentle and loving toward oneself and arm the mind with knowledge before it slowly can start to see the light of Truth. It takes many, many life experiences before answers are wanted, for release from what seems like a continuous nightmare. We must take a tremendous leap of faith to escape from this dream world.

## PLATO'S - THE ALLEGORY OF THE CAVE

The Allegory of the Cave should bring comprehension and clarity regarding the complexity of being caught up in an illusion, and the challenges of escaping from it. The conditioning of a prolonged belief system creates one's reality. These intensely held thoughts and beliefs create the imagined prisons within the mind which take on a life of their own. Once they are firmly established within the mind, it is extremely difficult to break free from thoughts that keep it imprisoned.

*Plato's Cave* was presented by the Greek philosopher *Plato* in his work *Republic.* [4] It is a metaphor of the human's condition, living within an illusion.

*Plato has Socrates describe a group of people who have lived chained to the wall of a cave all their lives, facing a blank wall. The people watch shadows projected on the wall, created by objects passing in front of a fire, which is behind them. They give these shadows names, thinking they are real people. The shadows become the prisoners' reality.*

*The inmates of this place do not desire to leave their prison for they have known no other life. One of the prisoners manages to break free one day and discovers that what they thought was true reality was not that at all. What they believed was the real world, was just a cave with a wall full of shadows.*

*He quickly went back to free the others, excitedly sharing his discovery of another reality and telling them that the world they were experiencing was only an illusion. They did not believe him and wanted to kill him. Fear of the shadow people continued to keep them prisoners in an illusionary world.*

The *light,* truth of one's Reality, symbolized by the fire behind the prisoners, cannot be observed because it is hidden. It is obscured by a false reality created by senses and conditioned beliefs within the mind, which keep the mind imprisoned in an illusionary state. The false reality with its ingrained driver of the experience, *fear,* is greatly misconstrued and misinterpreted. Like the prisoners, human beings have great difficulty in breaking free of the chains that bind them to this illusion.

Even when the mind can break free from bondage to this world, it discovers that it is a struggle to fully comprehend and embrace the *Light*. The beauty and perfection of the mind's True Reality, a world of unconditional love and peace, is completely unfathomable to the mind and extremely difficult to accept as Truth. Consequently, one may continue to choose to be a prisoner of this illusionary world.

# CHAPTER

# 12

# THE AWAKENING

*"Appearances deceive because they are appearances and not reality. Dwell not on them in any form. They but obscure reality, and they bring fear because they hide the truth....What could it be but an illusion, making things appear like to itself?....His one mistake is that he thinks them real. What can the power of illusions do?"*

ACIM [1]

The world is a thought imagined in the mind. Our universe is emptiness, just energy milling around, it is nothing! So how did this come about? Scientists and Physicists have spent eons of time speculating on the *Big Bang Theory*. If the *Big Bang Theory* is to be entertained; then, what caused the big bang and where did the mass come from? It has been a constant struggle to find the answer to that question.

*"The Bible says, "The Word (or thought) was made flesh." Strictly speaking this is impossible, since it seems to involve the translation of one order of reality into another. Different orders of reality merely appear to exist, just as different orders*

*of miracles do. Thought cannot be made into flesh except by belief, since thought is not physical." [2]*

Among many Physicists and Scientists there appears to be a variety of opinions regarding the universe. One opinion is that the universe had its beginnings quite possibly from *nothing*, no existence of time, space or matter. *Stephen Hawking* often speculated that the whole universe is a self-contained unit, with no awareness of what may have come before it. His suggestions were that it just *is* and cannot be created or destroyed. [3]

*"The all is mind; the universe is mental! Everything in the universe is created by thought. There is nothing that exists in the material universe in which this is not the case."[4]*

The universe, which is believed to be our reality, is simply the thought of an active mind, a creation of the mind. The key word is *mind*. The universe and everything in it only exists within the one sick mind. A sane mind could not have possibly created this world.

## WHAT IS "A COURSE IN MIRACLES?"

### *"I know you are tired but come, this is the way." [5]*

My journey through grief sent me down many paths in search of truth. The paths always led me back to one book. My niece was kind enough to allow me to borrow several books from her box of self-help books. Among them all, was this thick book which I picked up and put down a number of times, only to end up adding it to my pile. This book is called *A Course in Miracles*. Jesus dictated the context of this book.

*"A miracle is a correction. It does not create, nor really change at all. It merely looks on devastation, and reminds the mind that what it sees is false." [6]*

In the book called A *Course in Miracles, miracles* refers to corrections of perceptions of this universe and bodies that die. It's important to correct this thought system within the mind, so it could find its way back to its True Reality. It took many life experiences to get to this state of false belief and it requires a lot of work to disintegrate and deprogram all the falsehoods of that belief system.

Here is a brief description of how this book came about. *A Course in Miracles* [7] was transcribed by Helen Schucman and William Thetford, psychologists at the Columbia Presbyterian Medical Center in New York City. The personalities of the Psychologists within the Medical Center seemed to be in constant conflict. After several years of disharmony within the Psychology Department, one day, the head of the department suggested to Helen that he thought there had to be a better way of dealing with disruptive meetings and consequent problems. Helen agreed with him and expressed interest in helping to find another way.

Helen was in her fifties and a very militant atheist. She began to have psychic and mystical experiences both during the day and in her night dreams, where upon the figure of Jesus began to appear more and more regularly. Helen started to record her highly symbolic dreams. This was followed by her recording a *Voice*, that gave her a kind of rapid, inner dictation. This Voice introduced itself as the Voice of Jesus. Bill encouraged her to write it all down. She was very reluctant and wondered why she had been chosen for this task. The dictation took place over a span of seven years with a lot of work and help from Bill, resulted in three books in one called *A Course in Miracles.*

This course can therefore be summed up very simply in this way:

> *"Nothing real can be threatened.*
> *Nothing unreal exists.*
> *Herein lies the peace of God."* [8]

For those who think this world is real, these words may be difficult to believe, or even care to read. I was enthralled, even though initially, I could not comprehend the possibility of that Truth. Perhaps, there was a recognition of inner knowledge that caught my interest and would not release me. It was truly a relief for me to learn there was a life much better than this nightmare, I had been living. The book tells us, we are really all asleep, dreaming. It is time to wake up!

It took me nearly a year to read the 669-page Text, 488-page Workbook for Students, and 92-page Manual for Teachers. I read it again and did the daily lessons until I started to understand how it was possible that nothing that I saw existed. This was a form of deprogramming and stripping the false beliefs that have tied me to this world. It was the start of an unimaginable hunger for wisdom and a deep desire to comprehend many mysteries of this world.

While reading this book for the second time, I had an epiphany; I painfully became aware of an ecstatic truth. It was clear to me that the timing and circumstances of Steve's death along with the accompanying experience of intense inner pain, was all part of an unveiling of a colossal gift of love to me. I recognized that I was a recipient of an immeasurable gift, for which I felt deeply humbled and tremendously grateful. This event was the catalyst, the passionate driver of an incessant need for answers, turning my life in a completely different direction, a path toward awakening from this dream, my life's purpose.

## REOCCURRING DREAM

*"Life and death are one, even as the river and the sea are one. In the depths of your hopes and desires lies your silent knowledge of the beyond and like seeds dreaming beneath the snow, your heart dreams of spring. Trust the dreams, for in them is hidden the gate to eternity."*[9]

For many years, I had a reoccurring dream. Some of the dynamics of the dream would change, but the theme of the dream was always the same.

*I would be driving a car, always through chaotic traffic, and everyone would be driving insanely and in the opposite direction from me. Ultimately, I would end up being the only driver on a single-lane road, with water on either side of it for as far as the eye could see. I'd come to the end of the road where it would be completely cut off by water.*

*I'd get out of my car and just stand there, looking out into the abyss; the endless water melded into the misty, cloudy, and grey sky. There was such loneliness, emptiness, and longing in my heart, a sense of grief beyond description. I would just stand there, as though I was waiting and hoping for a hand to reach down, lift me up, and take me away. I'd wake up in a complete sweat and the emotional imprint of that dream would stay with me throughout the following days.*

A year or so after the passing of my husband, I had a similar dream, now with an infusion of clarity.

*The same theme, I was driving out of the city, down a road out into the country. There was water on either side of the road and unbelievable frenzied traffic coming toward me. This time there were not only cars and trucks, but also bikes, motorcycles, horses, buggies, people on foot running, families with babies, and crippled people trying to pass one another, crossing over to my side of the road.*

*I, too, was driving very fast and, once again, was the only one going in the opposite direction. I kept thinking to myself, "This is crazy, I need to get off this road before I end up killing someone." I decided that if and when I come to the next road that turned off to my right, I'd take that road.*

*Soon enough I came upon a road on my right and immediately made the turn, finding myself on a narrow country road with water on either side of it. Nevertheless, typical of a country dirt road there were some saplings of shrubs growing in the ditch, and I thought to myself, "Oh good, it will be easier for me to see exactly where the shoulders of the road are, so I won't drive off".*

*It wasn't long before I came to the part where the water completely covered the road. I could no longer see where the road was and, once again, all I could see was water blending into the misty grey that was very quickly enveloping everything around me. A dense opaque sheet was everywhere. I was going way too fast to stop. Shear panic gripped my whole body, as I raced forward, about to be swallowed by it.*

*The next thing I knew, I was in the back of my car, curling up with a soft down-pillow and a blanket pulled up to my neck, peacefully surrounded by unconditional love, feeling completely safe and protected. I drifted away into a much-needed sleep, thinking, "It is really comforting to know that Jesus is driving my car." I fell into the most profound, blissful and restful sleep!*

*Eventually, I woke up, completely refreshed, and proceeded to smoothly slip into the driver's seat. Looking out the window, the skies had cleared, and the sun was shining brightly. Ahead of me was what looked like a rest stop with a bunch of vehicles parked and people milling around. I came to an abrupt stop facing a big transfer truck.*

*I decided to pull into a proper parking spot among the cars. I parked my car and quickly threw open my door, running out - shouting, "Jesus was driving my car! Jesus was driving my car!" Everyone, including my deceased sister, abruptly turned away and retreated from me as quickly as possible.*

*No one listen! No one cared!*

I awoke from my dream in deep contemplation!

Reflecting upon what may have been a message of my repetitive dreams, I began to understand that *water* represented my unconscious mind. What I needed to overcome and heal was obscured and hidden. This all-encompassing massive body of pain was difficult to contain, and was preventing access to the wisdom beyond, drawing a veil of fog over the mystery of my true existence. I needed to bring all my wrong minded thinking and behavior out, to be exposed and healed, and ride the storm through to the *Light.*

My *vehicle* represented my *body,* which was to serve as a tool for learning. I realized that *Jesus* was to be the *driver* of my vehicle, the guidance system, my GPS. It was through A *Course in Miracles* that *Jesus* was to guide my journey Home. I was also aware that I may be alone on this journey and would have a difficult time sharing my wisdom, and others may turn away from me.

### *"If Light is in your heart, you will find your way"*[10]

There was a realization that the journey I was undertaking was contrary to what most human beings were willing to travel. Receiving any answers to the mysteries of life would require searching in a different direction, one that was completely opposite to conventional thinking.

My thirst for information and knowledge continued unabated. I reached for all books spiritually oriented and any information that could possibly explain to me what this world was about and who we are. Not all information resonated as my truth. I understood that discernment was important and my mind appeared to know what was acceptable or probable.

I persistently and actively worked on my ever-changing belief system. Working intensely on removing any blinders, questioning what I believed, dismissing, understanding, formulating, and reconstructing all that would shape and culminate in a belief, which would become my Truth. Nevertheless, it was A *Course in Miracles* that repeatedly drew me back. It was this book that would lead me on the rest of my journey.

In my flood-dream, my sister turning away from me, represented the possibility that my own family might question my different views, and maybe even my sanity. It was not going to be an easy journey. A *Course of Miracles* will be my constant companion, as I intend to continue to re-read and absorb the knowledge while integrating its wisdom into my daily life.

I could not have possibly comprehended the intense transformation that my thinking was about to undertake. My world, as I knew it, was turned upside down, decomposed, rearranged and reframed, as I came to an understanding that what at first boggled my mind now continues to heal it. Progressively, slowly, but surely, loosening the chains that bind me to this illusionary world.

# THE DARK NIGHT OF MY SOUL

*Here is where we've come to be.*
*Not anywhere, seemingly everywhere.*
*Masses, masses, coming and going.*
*There are so many here.*
*Near suffocating; no air - can't breathe!*
*No space - don't move.*
*No time - won't waste.*
*Where did they come from? They are me, you say?*
*Demons wait, ego's hate, luring, dragging through a door.*
*Can't go, won't go.*
*Hell - No More!*
*Wake up! Wake up!*

*No relief, no rest, so much pain.*
*So alone! So alone!*
*Don't belong here! Don't belong here!*
*Falling ....... falling ...... down ....... down ........ down.*

*Screaming, clawing, fingers bleeding, grasping!*
*Further ...... further.........further.*
*Tired, so tired!*

*Darkness, such darkness!*
*A glowing hand, reaching, reaching.*
*Hold on tight! Won't let go, never let go!*
*Lifting higher......... higher.........higher!*

*Spirit flying!*
*Light embracing!*
*Going Home!*
*Jesus is driving my car!*

# CHAPTER
# 13

# IS THIS WORLD AN ILLUSION?

*"Here is a world established that is sick and this the world the body's eyes perceive. Here are the sounds it hears, the voices that its ears were made to fear. Yet sights and sounds the body can perceive are meaningless. It cannot see nor hear. It does not know what seeing is; what listening is for. It is as little able to perceive as it can judge or understand or know. Its eyes are blind, its ears are deaf. It cannot think, and so it cannot have effects."*

ACIM[1]

This is the world we believe is real. The accumulated sensations and beliefs in the mind project intended experiences onto a body. A thought only follows the imagination of the mind. I (the mind) was wrestling with understanding why a mind that was made perfect, as an extension of the Creator, would be creating a world of hate and destruction. What caused such a mind to be delusional?

*"The miracle does not awaken you, but merely shows you who the dreamer is. It teaches you there is a choice of dreams while*

*you are still asleep .... The miracle established you dream a dream, and that its content is not true.....The miracle returns the cause of fear to you (the mind) who made it."* [2]

Our minds are having a dream of being a body and having a life in a world. While in this dream, we (the mind) can choose a different dream. Before we can do that, we need to understand how this world could be just a dream and a body merely a figure in the dream, not the dreamer of the dream. All the fear and wrong mindedness is not in the body, but in the mind that thinks it. A *miracle* occurs when we understand that the dream creating fear and distress is not real. Understanding how it is possible to create a world in the mind, makes changing the dream much easier.

## HOW DID BODIES AND UNIVERSE COME TO EXIST?

*"Into eternity, where all is one, there crept a tiny, mad idea, at which the Son of God remembered not to laugh. In his forgetting (to laugh) did the thought become a serious idea, and possibly of both accomplishment and real effects."* [3]

We are given this myth to help us grasp the concept of the original event. Our minds are not capable of integrating a complete comprehension of the absolute Truth. The Christ Mind, of which we are all a part, is an extension of the Mind of God. The Son of God had a thought, a *what if* thought. A *mad idea!* An idea of separating from the Essence to experience *specialness*, much like the story of the prodigal son in the Bible. This thought lasted only a split second and disappeared just as quickly. It was only a thought, fleeting like the many thoughts we believe we have in our heads. In and out, gone from mind, or maybe not?

Rather than laughing at such a preposterous idea, the Son of God took it seriously and believed that the thought of being separated from God had actually happened. This caused intense guilt, immediately followed by fear of God's anger. So, a *thought* of something happening, that didn't actually happen, transformed into a fear and guilt-based reality. This *thought* literally took on a life of its own.

The collective mind of the Son of God was now delusional, firmly believing that separation from God had indeed occurred. This guilt was deep and painful, and the mind needed to do something to get rid of it. The ego part of the mind, the part that was going insane with guilt, thought of a solution, put the blame elsewhere. The mind proceeded to project the guilt onto parts of itself, manifesting guilt into a form called a *body*, affirming that the separation from the Source actually happened. Similar to the Bible story about the prodigal son leaving his home.

None of this actually happened, neither the separation, or ego's existence. This is all just in a *thought* within the mind, *an imagined situation*. This illusionary self, ego, was an answer to the intense guilt felt when the mind believed the separation happened.

Nothing happened! The actual *mad idea* came and went, but a belief that it occurred still remains with us (fractured minds) and keeps us prisoners within this thought! This imaginary self, ego, who we think we are, has convinced the mind that this was real and there was trouble. The ego's solution of projecting the guilt onto a separate part of itself, absolved it of any responsibility. Each separated mind proceeded to continue to project the guilt outward onto other parts of Self, separating itself further. Each part refusing to be accountable for the *mad idea*.

The crazy world is now off and running. The idea of projecting the internal guilt out onto others caused the *Big Bang*, as it catapulted parts of the mind, the Self, into an imagined universe. All this in a lunatic attempt to get rid of an imagined guilt.

It is the same as when an extremely traumatic event causes the mind to fragment itself into two personalities. The mind disassociates itself from *Self*. It now believes it is two people rather than one. One which is loving and kind, the victim and innocent one; the other one is angry and vengeful. We perceive ourselves, as being the loving victim; the other is the horrible one, whose very existence is now our greatest burden. There isn't another actual person, it's still the same Self, but the mind *believes* it is another person. Duality is created out of one, the ego and the right mind or Higher Self.

What should be obvious now becomes obscured. It was less painful for the mind to accept that the pain was outside itself rather than within. The mind is now delusional. This illusionary world becomes a self-made prison, the door is locked, and the key is thrown away. Is it possible to *pick* that lock? Shall we at least try?

In an article printed in *New Scientist, 12 April 2008, p 26,* there are many theories stating that the Big Bang would have created matter and antimatter in equal amounts. [4] Keeping that in mind, the universe should have disappeared as soon as it appeared. That is exactly what happened. It never existed. Nevertheless, the mind *believes* it does exist. Rather than owning the extreme guilt and fear created by the *thought* - the *mad idea,* the mind keeps attempting to project guilt onto parts of itself, giving this universe continuous life.

Projection is what little kids do when they attempt to get rid of that - nose booger - off their finger by flinging it onto someone else. Then, that child flings it off onto someone else, and so on. "There, now it's your problem; you are the rude one and a nuisance to me." Another childhood favorite form of projection is farting and blaming a brother or a friend. "I didn't do it, Johnny did it! He is the stinky rotten person; I am the innocent one." No one wants to take responsibility for their own actions. It may be a crude way of explaining projection, but if the concept is more easily grasp by thinking of boogers and farts, then so be it!

This is a more classic example of projection. My deaf sister communicates via a fax machine. In one of her faxes, as she was trying to express herself, her words were getting muddled up. Instead of admitting that she seemed to be having trouble keeping her thoughts straight, she said, "My gel-pen seems to be getting confused."

It is always the fault of something or someone else. The mind continues to project blame onto parts of itself, further fragmenting itself in an attempt to get rid of guilt for something that never happened. Consequently, we believe when we feel hurt, sad, fearful or guilty, it is because of someone else. We don't accept the part we may have played in causing the situation. *They* are the cause of our miserable selves!

## IS THE UNIVERSE EXPANDING?

As time goes on, memory of the original cause is pushed further and further into the unconscious mind, denied and repressed, and filed away among ancient archives, under *useless information* and *unimportant.* The universe is continually expanding; the mind keeps separating itself. In a futile attempt to get rid of inner guilt, it projects it out on to other parts of itself, creating more bodies.

Scientists and Physicists debate and speculate whether the universe is expanding or contracting. As long as the mind refuses to accept responsibility for its choices and continues to fragment itself further to accommodate unprocessed guilt, the world will continue to expand.

I recently watched a *How the Universe Works* documentary in which Astrophysicists discussed an epic battle for control of the cosmos - dark matter verses dark energy, causing the universe to expand.[5] In an article in the *National Geographic*, the visible universe occupies 5%, dark matter 25%, and dark energy 70% of the total mass of the universe. There was overwhelming evidence that an abundance of dark energy, a repulsive force, was pushing dark matter further away - expanding the universe.[6]

Until the mind decides to question the cruelty of this world and desire things to be different, it will continue to imprison itself in the illusionary world. We simply forgot to laugh! The Truth is that the Christ Mind, in which all the fragmented parts of the whole are still whole, is fast asleep and dreaming of exile. The big problem remains in the fact that the fractured parts of the mind actually *believe they are a body* in this *guilt* created world.

*"The world you see depicts exactly what you thought you did. Except that now you think that what you did is being done to you. The guilt for what you thought is being placed outside yourself, and on a guilty world that dreams your dreams and thinks your thoughts instead of you. It brings its vengeance, not your own. It keeps you narrowly confined within a body, which it punishes because of all the sinful things the body does within its dream. You have no power to make the body stop its evil deeds because you did not make it, and cannot control its actions nor its purpose nor its fate."* [7]

The mind's belief that *it* is a *body* and as a *body* is responsible for everything that happens in this world is completely false. The mind is the creator and the director of this dream-world and has the power to change the script at any time. Everything that we think is outside of us in our world, is really inside of the sick mind. We are not the body, we are the *sick mind*.

The world is the mind's mirror. The initial projection of the mind's guilt did not go anywhere. It rears its ugly head over and over again. So everyone's mind keeps projecting it onto others, fragmenting itself more and more. The body is powerless. It is merely a symbol of guilt. The mind is continually trying to rid itself of something that never happened. It endlessly punishes the body and other bodies, believing it is justified; the truth is, it is punishing itself by furthering fragmentation of itself.

This world is one long continuous nightmare. No one is guilty of anything. We live in a world of illusions. Everything done in this illusion is still an illusion. It is not real. An illusionary body cannot do anything to hurt another illusionary body. It is just an imaginary thought in a SICK MIND!

The Creator, or God, is aware that the Son of God is sleeping in the True Reality. He is also aware of the dream the Christ Mind is having. God is lovingly waiting for the Son of God to awaken. *God does not enter the dream, since to do so would make it real.* It is not real! *The event and everything in the universe was not created by God; it was created by the delusional mind.*

## WHAT IS THE HOLY SPIRIT?

*"The Holy Spirit abides in the part of your mind that is a part of the Christ Mind. He represents your Self and your Creator, Who are One. He speaks for God and also for you, being joined with Both."*[8]

Because the separated mind believes separation did indeed occur and the universe is real, God sent a messenger into the dream, into the illusion. This messenger goes by the name of *Higher Self, Holy Spirit* or *Jesus* who is a manifestation of the *Holy Spirit.* The Holy Spirit is the source of communication between God (Essence) and his separated Sons (fragmented mind), between the Truth and the illusion. The Holy Spirit is our connecting link to God. Either one, Holy Spirit, Higher Self, Jesus, or Right-mindedness could be considered the interpreter, translator or direct line of communication between us (mind) and God. This is the *Voice* for God.

*"He is the great correction principle; the bringer of true perception, the inherent power of the vision of Christ. He is the light in which the forgiven world is perceived; in which the face of Christ alone is seen. He never forgets the Creator or His creation. He never forgets the Son of God. He never forgets you. And He brings the Love of your Father to you in an eternal shining that will never be obliterated because God has put it there."*[9]

The Holy Spirit is always within reach, whenever the mind chooses spiritual help. It's a desire to turn negative thoughts, beliefs, behaviors, and hate into Love. Understanding that forgiveness is the way back from insane beliefs of sin, is essential in order to embrace your eternal innocence. Forgiveness is the key to awakening from this nightmarish dream. It is the choice for right mindedness, wisdom, and total comprehension of one's True Reality.

It is essential to heal the mind of many false beliefs that have been imbedded over ages, understand that all are guiltless in a dream. Instead of continuing to be caught within this dream/illusion and the birth and death cycle, one must learn to step out and heal untruths, so clear vision would be restored to the mind. The body is; then, utilized as a learning tool to bring sanity to the mind. The Holy Spirit leads you to a path that will heal and awaken the mind to the Eternal Truth - your true being - the Christ-Mind, Eternally in Heaven.

CHAPTER

# 14

# GOING AGAINST THE CURRENT!

*"Many people especially ignorant people want to punish you for speaking the truth, for being correct, for being you. Never apologize for being correct or for being years ahead of your time. If you're right and you know it, speak your mind. Even if you are a minority of one, the truth is still the Truth."*

## MAHATMA GANDHI

A profound inner knowing always brings one back to center; a deeper commitment is made when, by chance, one opens a book and words of encouragement present themselves. It is a resounding confirmation that one is indeed on the right path toward Truth. I was consumed with wanting to understand the reasons behind all the perceived suffering in this world.

### ASTROLOGY - ENERGETIC GUIDANCE

Contrary to popular belief, human beings (thought-creations of the ego mind) are not wandering around aimlessly in this world. We (parts of the fractured mind) are not alone on this journey. Along with gifts of wisdom available and attainable through energetic Spiritual Caches strategically placed within the physical body, there are many energies activated at the very second of the birth of a body. There are various forms of GPS systems programmed, as a gentle guidance system, always coercing the mind to entertain other ways. Astrological studies of a personality's chart with exact time of birth, can provide an extended overview of probable negative twists and turns of one's life's journey, representing many opportunities available to make positive changes. It is a study of the planetary system's influences on the mind within the cycle of life.

Like seasons of the year, there are also seasons of life. In everything that exists in this dream world there's an endless cycle of birth and death. Everything in this universe is made of energy and is always in motion, including the cosmos. One planet's energy differs in intensity and quality in relation to another. They are continually either interfering, or are in harmony and assisting each other towards an intended particular result or conclusion. How the energy influences the mind's thinking, depends on whether planets are spinning in a forward, progressive movement, or in a backward, retrograde movement. Their position within the map of the cosmos, along with their relationships and placement in one's natal astrological chart can exert a tremendous amount of beneficial energy on the mind.

There may be times planets provide a boost of energy, or a draining of energy, a constant push or pull, assisting or resisting. There may be a call to action, to search deep within, to heal and let go, or take time to rest. Whether the mind is provided with clarity of thought, or if there appears to be a vague distortion in thinking, it is all a part of the script. Some of these energies could be subtle nudges, or a call for action, "Hello, time to act! Change your path and choose again!" Sickness or a car accident is a good wake-up call. All these influences are precisely and perfectly timed to create a particular effect with an intent of guiding and assisting the mind's healing. Continuous energies gently encourage forward movement, assisting with fulfilling the intended purpose for coming into this world at this time and place.

Just like Jesus, our brother, every one of us is also born with the *sun* sign strategically placed within the cosmic circle of life. The *sun* represents one's fullest potential which is the *heart center* of Love. The sign under which everyone is individually born, is appointed with wise precision, potent positioning and timing for optimum receptivity of intended gifts of energies from the interplay of different planets, stars, and asteroids. The time and place of our arrival into this world is uniquely timed and synchronized with these universal energies.

The *sun sign* is center of a fragmented mind's existence in this world. Just like the universal sun provides heat, light and nourishment for growth, the same is true of our *inner* sun. Unfortunately, most of us are not aware of our inner sun. In order to tap into the energy of our *sun* we must go within the mind and connect with the inner *Light*, which is an inner knowing, the *Higher Self*. The mind needs to be stripped of all ego masks and untruths of its belief system.

There is controversy regarding the *brilliant star* of Bethlehem, as well as the actual time and date of Jesus' birth. It has been mentioned in past-life regressions that there were three planets, or stars whose paths were crossing, which would certainly be an unusual event and a cause for combined brilliant display of light. Whether it is all symbolic or a myth, it gives fodder for a lot of speculation. It is difficult to know anything for sure within this illusion, other than everything is still just an illusion.

The three wise men from the birth story are symbolic of the Trinity of God:

*Christ - Son of God, Christ-Mind - which is our True Reality.*
The gift of gold (alchemy) - transmuting lead - worldly existence - to gold, representing Divine Kingship.

*Holy Spirit - communicator between Father and Sleeping Son.*
The gift of frankincense (an oil used for mind expansion) representing Spiritual wisdom - Enlightenment.

*God, Father, Source, Essence, Creator.*
The gift of myrrh (used for embalmment) representing Eternal life.

These gifts were not only for our brother Jesus, but also for all the other fractured minds believing they are bodies in this illusionary world. Through expanding our minds and becoming enlightened, there comes a discovery of our True Reality, the Son of God, the Christ-Mind and Eternal life.

So rather than a journey being one of becoming, it is a journey of rediscovering one's Self. The stripping away of multiple layers of guilt placed on the body, a symbol of guilt, to reveal a pure, innocent Spirit within the confused and fractured mind.

Let us just assume we have all been around the zodiac wheel of life many times, perhaps most times gaining nothing, as per the mind's will of choice. There are no limitations to one's growth potentiality, or the quickening of the awakening process. The only limitations existing are in the mind. It is essential to work diligently on the forgiveness process, so the consequential spiritual growth will expediently accelerate the evolution of one's Soul.

It is easy to fall back on old habitual behaviors. Nevertheless, the energetic divinely orchestrated dance is relentless. Sooner or later, depending on choices, one will arrive at the appointed destination. All the energies of the cosmos are gifts of potential movements within the rhythm of your mind's personal dance of life.

The end is certain. It is already complete. Steve's Spirit said, "It is only a moment in time." To us it feels like an eternity. So, if it's a done deal, why do we have to do anything? Well, one could go along as usual and eventually get to the finishing line and awaken; however, be prepared for a bumpy ride. You will have many opportunities to cruise over the bumpy ride, not only changing your future, but also your children's future and eliminate hundreds of birth and death cycles along with the accompanying pain that is often experienced. The journey can either be changed, shortened or not, the destination; however, is certain and unalterable.

# AUTOMATIC WRITING - SPIRIT COMMUNICATION

From time to time I would communicate with my Guides through automatic writing, expressing my fears, concerns, and desperations. My Spirit Helpers would always respond. What follows is one of those communications, which may reflect the frustrations you may be feeling right now, trying to integrate all this information.

Holy Spirit, you know my needs. I know in my heart this world is not real, I know everyone is me, yet I see separation everywhere. I see their confusion, pain, an inability to release it, and the futility of all disharmony. I see it all, why can I not see it is unreal? Why can I not heal my perceptions? I ask for help for true and clear vision. I know the bodies are not real, the perceived infractions and attacks are not real and yet I cannot see the *Light*, which is real! I struggle to understand, I struggle to heal, it's all elusive.

My thoughts keep giving me concern of not letting go. I see pain in parts of myself being caught up in a web unable to be released. Holy Spirit decide for me. I choose peace instead of this. I choose *Light* instead of this. Let there be *Light*, so the world would heal and release all untruths.

**Response:** *You cannot remain in this state of limbo you must transgress and move above this pain, so that all can heal. The world is not lost to pain and disharmony. You can save yourself, which is the world. The frustration and confusion is yours. The depression is your vision reflected back to you. Go past your mind's eyes and understand the Truth. Do not be fooled in believing it is real. The end is written, there is nothing you need do to intervene, or to change the end. Allow the Holy Spirit to finish directing the play, don't keep getting sucked into it.*

It's my projection, so that's it - what is inside of my mind needs to change, so that I could project it out onto the world I see. There is no one else just me.

**Response:** *The play continues, the cry for Love is from you. Be in knowing that it is being addressed, it will change if you see the change in you. See only goodness in you and it will be reflected in everything around you. What was your responsibility? What is asked of you?*

I don't know! Please tell me! I learned that indeed the world is sound asleep with no one desiring to wake up! Yet I desperately want to wake up - please help me to wake up! It's confusing, the world is me, how do I understand this?

**Response:** *You are not here to change the world, you are here to change the way you look at the world. Change yourself and the world will change with you.*

## PAPER-DOLL WORLD

*"What if you recognized this world is an hallucination? What if you really understood you made it up? What if you realized that those who seem to walk about in it, to sin and die, attack and murder and destroy themselves, are wholly unreal?*[1]

When I was a child, I never had many toys, a hand-me-down doll, perhaps. I spent a lot of time cutting out paper people, clothes, and furniture out of old Sears and Eaton's catalogues. I gave them all names and a life with roles they played. Complete with families, furnished houses, and neighbours within a world of paper and imagination. I produced their lives and put words in their mouths, expressed feelings, emotions, and conversations. There was an interplay of characters, while on their many life adventures. Some good and some bad people, joy, sadness, anger, and grief. I was playing the role of many. No one else was involved in this world. I would change the script whenever I wanted to.

All of this was created within the imagination in the mind. Of course, it was not real! The paper people had no power, no say, no decisions, no life, they were nothing! Nothing more than just a thought within the mind. I thought that I, the body made it up, but it was the mind that imagined itself to be a body, that made it up. Are bodies the paper people?

*"The all is mind, the universe is mental. This principle embodies the understanding that everything in the universe is created by the thought or mind. There is nothing that exists in the material universe where this is not the case".*[2]

The mind is thinking that if it makes the body a scapegoat and the cause of all problems, it doesn't need to take responsibility for its own decisions. We, as a body, don't make *any* choices, the body does what the mind tells it to do. The body cannot *sin*, nor does it have free will. As a body, we do nothing. It is the mind's sick thinking that materializes in the imagined body as sickness. To try to cure the body of sickness is ridiculous. The mind needs to be healed. The body is not the cause of the problems, it is the effect of the sickness within the mind, which is the cause of this nightmarish world we so cherish.

Our bodies and everything else in this world, eventually dies, disintegrates, returns to molecules, atoms, and energy. This energy all changes back to other compositions of matter. We are forever breathing and eating the same energy that once was the composition of other bodies. We are created from the interchanging energy of other bodies and life forms in this world. Nothing is permanent, everything is constantly changing.

Since the mind believes it exists in a body and a world that is real, it will continue to be trapped within the birth and death cycle. The right-mindedness needs to take control. The ego-mind will do everything it can to make this world real, its very existence depends on it. Once you decide to choose another way, be prepared to be continually sucked back into this illusionary world. If you remain steadfast and aware that it is still *an illusionary world* no matter what the ego throws at your life experience, you will overcome it all.

## IS THERE VALUE IN WHAT IS VALUELESS?

*"Each thing you value here is but a chain that binds you to the world, and it will serve no other end but this."*[3]

To say my ego did not give me a good fight in trying to convince me that the body and material things were valuable and worthy of my attachment to this world, is a gross understatement. I was never overly extravagant. I certainly wasn't rolling in money, so my purchases were on a modest level. Like everyone else, I worked hard to be able to purchase things and pay for the many other material entrapments of this world. I did enjoy shopping, usually buying just what I didn't need, and what didn't really make me happy. None the less, there was a need to learn through life's lessons, what was valuable and what was not.

I bought a new car a few years after my husband's death. I was proud of my ability to do so and was determined to keep it in mint condition. One evening, while attending a course on spirituality, my car was broken into. Two dollars of loose change and a cooler full of groceries was stolen. A window was broken, causing approximately two thousand dollars worth of damage. One of my questions was, "Why did this happen *to* me?" The truth was that it happened *for* me.

It took a couple of months in an auto-body shop to get the repair done, this included fixing a side door which required repairing and painting. I went to pick it up late in the day and by the time I got there it was getting dark, so I refused to sign the completed job sheet. I said I wanted to look at the repairs in day light because even in the dark, I noticed that the paint job was not up to acceptable standards.

The owner, a big burly man, got extremely angry and proceeded to intimidate me by slamming things down, screaming at me, belittling me, and refusing to give me my keys unless I signed the satisfactory-job release document. We were alone in the building; all other staff left for the day. An overpowering feeling of fear swept through me, as I tried desperately to steady my shaking hand and attempted to dial 911 for help. When he realized what I was trying to do, he very reluctantly gave me my keys.

I left there completely traumatised. Feeling extremely vulnerable, I recall lamenting, "How do I find the strength to stand in my own power?" I filed a complaint with the insurance company asking for a re-assessment. Upon agreeing with my concerns, the insurance company complied. I took my car to a different auto-body shop. Two months later, the job was finally completed.

I did learn to assert myself and managed to somewhat stand in my power. Sadly, however, my car had now decreased in value. Certainly monetarily, but also because of all the emotional trauma attached to it, the car was not so dear to me anymore.

One day when I stopped at my son's home, their family dog managed to squeeze by me and ran out the door. She ran to the car to find the rest of family and proceeded to jump up on both sides of the car, scratching the paint all the way down. I love the dog and knew she meant no harm, so I tried to polish off the scratches. Thinking, "Oh well, it is now what it is!"

A year later, while taking my sister out for a day of shopping, I parked at the end of the parking lot, as I normally did still trying to avoid door-dings. At the end of the day, as I was driving out of a parking lot, my car was hit by another vehicle. I was shocked, confused, and once again distressed.

Approximately three thousand dollars later, and a year and half of attempting to get it properly fixed including the damage done, while on the parking lot of the auto-body compound, it was finally repaired. My once prized possession was now completely tainted by thought induced worry, anxiety, fear, guilt, and total disharmony. Through these experiences I have been able to re-align my beliefs to reflect what is truly valuable and what is not.

Being the youngest of ten children, I was accustomed to hand-me down clothing and just a few remnants of toys, which I lovingly recreated, giving them new life. Throughout my adult life, I enjoyed shopping at second-hand stores, so my attachments to materialistic things took on a different twist from the accepted norm of society. Any association to materialistic gifts had very little to do with the value of the things and more to do with the value of the underlying love of the act of giving, which would be drawn into my heart for safe keeping.

There were many life lessons greatly loosening my ties to the material world. Everything in this world will disintegrate, decompose, and we will leave the same way we came in to this world with nothing, butt naked, and probable some of us will still be screaming. I know my screams will be of joy.

## LUCID DREAM

*"Can you paint rosy lips upon a skeleton, dress it in loveliness, pet it and pamper it, and make it live? And can you be content with an illusion that you are living?"*[4]

We could try to paint the body and dress it in beautiful clothing with shiny trinkets and make it attractive, but is it really alive? Does it bring us permanent joy, total love and peace? At this point of my life, I became concerned about moving ahead with my spiritual journey, realizing that my family was not remotely interested in riding along with me. I was distraught and disheartened about possibly leaving them behind. Even though, I knew they were not their bodies, I felt conflicted and struggled with emotional pain, as if I was grieving for their loss.

I was concerned that I would be abandoning my loved ones, by fully integrating the new-found Truth into my mind. How could all that I greatly valued be valueless? I begged my Spirit Guides to help me move beyond this *mental* block and my ongoing battle with the ego. True to all of my spiritual communications, help did come to me, once again, in a lucid dream.

*The dream started rather confusingly, as most dreams do; however, clarity came when I became aware of entering what appeared to be a big city intersection. My body seemed to be just standing there looking around. I was the observer of the body and I was the body observed. My attention was drawn to my left where there was a large gathering of thousands of people. They were all completely naked. I stood there observing many shapes, sizes, ages and conditions of bodies, along with different facets of human behavior.*

*This, very quickly, turned into a horror movie on "speed", totally out of control; a torrent of gruesome and abhorrent images. There were ugly arguments, screaming, vulgarity, jealousy, bulling, hate, anger, fighting, and murder followed by intense suffering and grieving. A wide range of repugnant and deplorable behavior, in its fullest and most vivid expression. Complete mayhem!*

*I stood there watching, disgusted, repulsed, nauseated, and completely horrified by how ugly the body compounded by human behavior really was. I was asked through "thought-transfer", "Is this what you are resisting in letting go? Choosing this life rather than heavenly beauty beyond description where only peace and love exist?"*

Upon awakening, I lay in bed in deep reflection, knowing emphatically, that I was no longer attracted to anything in this world. What I thought was valuable, was now seen as revolting and undesirable.

What was revealed to me was an overwhelming understanding of the ego's ability to zone in on the mind's insecurities and vulnerabilities caused by the initial guilt of separation. To be able to bait the mind's thought system with many worldly distractions and greatly desired material things. The use of beautiful clothes, jewelry, and make-up with an intended purpose to cover up the truth of the body. A body was created a symbol of guilt!

Ego creates pretenses and false personalities with layers of masks; it weaves its many webs of deception to make the body and world, irresistible to the mind. If the mind is still not completely hooked, the ego taps into the mind's constant need to fill the ever present happiness void, by seducing it with new materialistic trends and *got to have it* mentality.

All this to lure, seduce, and entrap the mind in this world. How cleverly it obscures its hidden weapons, tools of the ego, as it masterfully disguises the ugliness which lies beneath all materialistic entrapments, all the pain, fear, hate, and guilt.

The willing mind now in a trance-like sleep-walking state, follows the other sheep (fractured minds) to the slaughter, focused and led only by a carrot full of eons of believed untruths which are blindly accepted. The ego continues to reel in and sink the mind further and further into the illusion, never questioning. This is the body and world we cherish!

*"It might be worth a little time to think once about the value of this world. Perhaps you will concede there is no loss in letting go all thought of value here. The world you see is merciless indeed, unstable, cruel, unconcerned with you, quick to avenge and pitiless with hate. It gives but to rescind, and takes away all things that you have cherished for a while. No lasting love is found, for none is here. This is the world of time, where all things end."*[5]

It was imperative for me to take a long hard unbiased appraisal of this world. I reflected upon my past attachments to all I found valuable. My childhood was spent mostly in solitude, where value was found in nature and in the invisible. I spent most of my young life trying to find acceptance, belonging, and love. Love was always conditional and very fleeting.

I couldn't understand the rules, or laws of the planet that needed to be obeyed to find a space where I felt I belonged. A lot of time was spent trying to mimic behaviors of others, hoping I would figure out the secret to true love and happiness. Most of the time, all would go terribly wrong; what worked for others did not work for me.

I have been personally exposed to many factions of human behavior and expressions and not really finding many of them satisfactory, appealing, or worth retaining. I spent much of my adult life in isolation, conforming to other's expectations in an attempt to fulfill a requirement that was acceptable to them. Tremendous emotional pain was my frequent companion, as I cried in desperation, wanting a way out of this cruel and loveless world.

Is there anything in this world worthy of keeping? Only unconditional love is real and worthy of keeping and that kind of love cannot be found here. My children and grandchildren are not my children, they are Spirits trying to make their way Home, just like me. Of course, I love them as unconditionally as possible in this world, and they are the goodness that often times sustain me. The Spirits that play the role of my children will one day also become aware they are not their bodies, as they travel on this same journey. My children are part of the same Christ Mind as I am, so one day we will not only be within reach, but within Love itself, the most peaceful and loving place possible, eternally.

I am completely certain, that this world is not a place where anything of permanent value can be found. What this world has taught me is that it holds no value, other than to serve as a school in which to learn of our Truth, so we would awaken from this dream. We don't belong here and what we all are, and will always be, is not of this world. It is time we come to realize that what is valuable is our True Reality. We are Eternal. We are LOVE.

# CHILDREN

*Your children are not your children. They are the sons and daughters of Life's longing for Self. They come though you but not from you. And though they are with you, yet they belong not to you. You may give them your love, but not your thoughts. For they have their own thoughts.*

*You may house their bodies, but not their Souls. For their Souls dwell in the house of tomorrow, which you cannot visit not even in your dreams. You may strive to be like them seek not to make them like you. For life goes not backwards nor tarries with yesterday.*

*You are the bows from which your children, as living arrows are sent forth. The archer sees the mark upon the path of infinite and He bends you with His might that His arrows may go swift and far. Let your bending in the archer's hand be for gladness; for even as He loves the arrow that flies, so He loves also the bow that is stable.*

The Prophet - Kahlil Gibran[6]

# CHAPTER
# 15

# HOW DOES ONE HEAL
# THE MIND?

*"Forgiveness ends the dream of conflict here. Conflict must be resolved. It cannot be evaded, set aside, denied, disguised, seen somewhere else, called by another name, or hidden by deceit of any kind, if it would be escaped. It must be seen exactly as it is, where it is thought to be, in the reality which has been given it, and with the purpose that the mind accorded it. For only then are its defenses lifted, and the truth can shine upon it as it disappears."*

ACIM[1]

What we admire or despise in others are the same attributes that lie deeply hided in our unconscious mind. Ego comes to the rescue, projecting the guilt, fear, and anger onto someone else, temporarily making the problem *out there* rather than *within*. We accuse others of what lives deep in our minds. On a conscious level we are not aware of it and are convinced we do not have a problem, the problem lies in others. It will remain in our mind, no matter how many times we try to depress, deny, or project it onto others in a futile attempt to get rid of it.

The problem does not go anywhere. It repeatedly shows up in our day to day lives appearing to be outside of ourselves; it is in full view, the elephant in the room. Our sight is obscured by guilt and fear in our mind. We ask, "Why does this keep happening to us?" It keeps happening *for* us, so we might recognize it and take ownership of the fact that it is inside of our mind, until then, the world will keep mirroring it back to us. The unconscious mind continually seeks to heal itself.

Since we insist on projecting the problem outwards, we suffer consequent stresses that are caused by its repetitive reappearance in our outside world. We spend lifetimes repeating that same pattern, attacking and blaming others. "You did this to me, you are the problem, it is with you, not with me. If it weren't for you, my life would be fine." Even if we remove ourselves from that person, someone else will show up to fill that role. We just recycle all of them.

All our relationships are special. They are opportunities to heal our minds. When the drama subsides, and one can reflect inward, intensely personal questions need to be asked. The most powerful work is done in our day to day interactions. This is also the time ego has the upper hand in controlling situations. Intense emotional interactions are its domain. Created solely to continue the problematic life we all lead in this world. There is always a problem, which needs to be worried about and dealt with. That is the name of this game, called life.

When we find ourselves reacting, or affected emotionally by any issue in our outside world, it is an indication to us that it is our *stuff*. If you spot it, you've got it. Use that opportunity to own it and heal it. This concept is not easy to integrate into our daily lives. At times, the drama is too intense, and it is difficult to step back to remove yourself from the scene and be the observer rather than the active participant.

Within the diverse dynamics of relationships we learn that everyone is really one. What is imperative is that when we look at the other face, we see our own. Once we are aware of this truth, we can better understand that the disharmony we see in others is really inside of us. It is the guilt and pain that has caused sickness in the mind since the beginning of time.

## TAKE OWNERSHIP OF OUR STUFF

*"Forgiveness paints a picture of a world where suffering is over, loss becomes impossible and anger makes no sense. Attack is gone, and madness has an end. What suffering is now conceivable? What loss can be sustained? The world becomes a place of joy, abundance, charity and endless giving."[2]*

To take responsibility for your stuff, start by asking, "What is it I am supposed to learn from this?" Start peeling the layers of the onion, layers of false thinking. Keep peeling it back, until you get to the last emotion you are hanging on to, face it, address it, forgive yourself and others, and heal your mind.

Think back to a situation when you hurt someone. See the scene in your mind and ask yourself, "What emotion was I feeling?" If it is anger, remember that the face you directed your anger to was really your own. Imagine yourself looking at your image in a mirror. You were angry at you. Why were you angry at you? What issues do you refuse to address that are inside of your mind? What do you think you did that was so terrible you can't be forgiven?

Slowly, look at the emotion underneath the anger, what's underneath that? Sadness perhaps? Why are you so sad? What happened that caused you to be sad? Is there guilt beneath the sadness? What do you feel guilty about? What's underneath that? Rejection? Who did you reject? Your True Self perhaps?

There is no room for denial or pretention. Remember it is *your* face disguised as another face. When you become aware of the truth, feel the act, go through the pain, forgive, and let it go. Know that it is okay. You did what you felt you needed to do at the time, you didn't know any better. Ask the Holy Spirit to help you, forgive yourself and others, let go of the emotional baggage, take the learning instead and move forward. Most importantly, it wasn't real. Nothing really happens in an illusionary world. No one is guilty of anything. Forgive yourself for believing it was real.

*"When you feel the holiness of your relationship is threatened by anything, stop instantly and offer the Holy Spirit your willingness, in spite of fear, to let Him exchange this instant for the holy one you would rather have. He will never fail in this."*[3]

The mind cannot do this alone and the ego will continue to misdirect you. If there is difficulty in believing any of this, *fake it until you make it.* Simply go through the motions of the process. One needs to specifically ask the Holy Spirit to intervene and handle the situation. Do not question its guidance, flow with it gracefully and trust completely. Remember the ego speaks first, the Holy Spirit speaks second. Listen to the second voice. It is by choosing with the *Higher Self/Holy Spirit*, we will be able to heal and move up the evolutionary ladder.

## WHAT IS FORGIVENESS?

*"Condemn and you are made a prisoner. Forgive and you are freed. Such is the law that rules perception."*[4]

How do we heal this guilt? Intellectual understanding is not enough. It took many, many lifetimes to create the false belief that *this world is real.* We need to deprogram the mind. Strip the many layers of conditioning and forgive. Forgiveness of any kind is always welcomed; however, it can easily become sinister in nature if directed by one's ego.

That kind of forgiveness gives the ego a sense of superiority. You are the better of the people involved, forgiving out of kindness of your heart because you are wonderful, and they are not. "You hurt me, but I am *holier than thou* and so I forgive you." Or by playing the martyr, "How good am I who, with the patience of a saint, endured the pain, anger, and hurt you inflicted upon me, but do not show it. Instead I rise above you to forgive you." Or strike a deal, "I will forgive, but you'll need to suck up to me and worship my every step, and it better not happen again." Rather than being truly forgiven, one is now indebted forever in return for your absolution.

## THE ACT OF FORGIVENESS

*"I have indeed misunderstood the world because I laid my sins on it and saw them looking back at me. How fierce they seemed! And how deceived was I to think that what I feared was in the world instead of in my mind alone."* [5]

We see our own *sins* in everyone else that is in our world. That is where we project them because we don't want to see them in ourselves. In truth, when we forgive someone else, we are forgiving ourselves. Try to see beyond the body to understand that everyone is you, a sleeping - Son of God. Your vision is obscured and distorted by your false beliefs; you are one, seen as many. Greet them with holiness and equality. **Let me be clear: there are no such things as *sins*; there are only mistakes.**

The ugliness you see outside of yourself is only inside your unconscious mind. Conversely, the goodness you see outside yourself is equally inside you. What you extend to others is returned to you; the mirror will be reflecting it back and all around you. Forgiveness is the gentle slow release of the chains that bind one to this world, healing the mind and slowly awakening from this dream.

Ask the *Holy Spirit/Higher Self* to help you because your mind still believes that you and others are separated bodies. The mind is frightened and sick with guilt, for separating from God. It was tricked into believing this world is real. Ask to heal your mind and to assist your mind in understanding that *everyone* is guiltless. The truth is that nothing happened, it is not real.

Until you are able to see through the world and see the illusions without any hesitation, know that there is still inner healing to be done. You have not yet been able to awaken completely to the truth because of negative blocks remaining in your unconscious mind. Your vision will still be obscured. It is a lifelong process. Don't take too much time to start the healing.

## FEELING THE PAIN OF REJECTION

*"Forgiveness is a choice. I never see my brother as he is, for that is far beyond perception. What I see in him is merely what I wish to see, because it stands for what I want to be the truth. It is to this alone that I respond, however much I seem to be impelled by outside happenings. I choose to see what I would look upon, and this I see, and only this. My brother's sinlessness shows me that I would look upon my own. And I will see it, having chosen to behold my brother in its holy light."* [6]

Throughout my life, there were many situations when I felt a deep sense of rejection. I needed to go within and start peeling back the onion of my emotional pain.

Why did I feel hurt? Who did I hurt? Throughout my lifetimes I am sure I consciously and unconsciously hurt many people. I'm aware that I was looking in a mirror, the image I saw was *mine*. Why did I hurt me? Was my mind's need to feel needed and loved, allowing others to take advantage of me? Was it still important for my mind to have others love me? What did my mind do that was so terrible that it felt unworthy of love?

I felt angry. It was my face I was looking at. Why was I angry at myself? I felt angry because I was deceived. The others that deceived me were really me. Who did I deceive? I deceived myself. I believed I was unlovable.

I felt sad. What did I do to make me feel sad? Could it be that my mind wanted to be special and wanted to be a part of other people's lives, to belong? I felt so all alone. Sadness consumed me. My mind was mistaken, who I really am, never was, is, or will ever be separated or alone. I continued to strip the layers of emotional pain.

I felt guilt. First, I thought my friends were guilty of hurting me, but they were my mirror. The guilt was inside me. I felt guilty for making them my scapegoats. Why did *I* feel guilt? Guilt is the driver of all of the fractured pieces of the mind (mankind). The guilt of making the choice of an existence separate from *the Source*.

The last emotion was rejection. I felt rejected. Who did I reject? I did some intense soul searching and realized that *rejection* was a common theme replaying itself in my life. This was mirrored to me many times, but I did not see my reflection. Why was I rejecting me? My mind was rejecting itself because it did not deserve to belong to the True Reality. Who did I reject? I rejected God, when I chose to separate.

Intense pain shot through my heart and Soul; unbearable home-sickness grasped my whole being, as I cried for the *Holy Spirit* to heal my mind. I asked for help to *forgive* myself and others, to give my mind true vision so it could awaken from this nightmare. I forgave my friends and myself for thinking they were bodies. I forgave myself, for believing that I was a body and this world was real. I asked the *Holy Spirit* to forgive us all, heal my mind and help me to clearly see - everyone - *guiltless*.

The truth is that my mind did not separate from God. NO-THING happened. It was just a *thought*, which disappeared as fast as it came. The mind was mistaken. There is nothing to feel guilty about and nothing to forgive! It is this kind of *forgiveness* that will be our Soul's redemption. I thanked the *Holy Spirit* for helping me understand that my friends did nothing to hurt me. None of this is real.

Rejection may still rear its ugly head. Perhaps it will have less and less of an emotional impact on my mind, at which time, it will clearly see through the illusion. I need to be vigilant and aware of these opportunities, continue to ask the *Holy Spirit* to heal my mind and help it understand that everyone is guiltless. Since everyone is me and if I am guiltless, from the prospective of my fractured mind so is everyone else that is in my life, my world. Nothing ever happened!

Is my mind totally healed? Unfortunately, there are many hurts, misconceptions, false beliefs compounded and layered, going back many lifetimes that need to be uncovered, understood, and healed. I am sure there will be plenty of opportunities to do so, again, and again, and still again.

In day to day activities there are often many choices that need to be made. All have two voices from which to choose; the first voice you hear will always be the ego, the second voice will be that of the Holy Spirit or your Higher Self. Choose the second voice; then, you will be on the direct path Home.

## SEEING MYSELF IN THE MIRROR

*"Today we hear a single Voice which speaks to us of truth, where all illusions end and peace returns to the eternal, quiet home of God."*[7]

One of the situations bringing my attention to my unconscious projections, was one involving the idea of writing a book. Many synchronistic events occurred. The idea - write a book - kept popping in and out of my awareness. The thought grew until I started to consider it. I dismissed it many times with self-defeating thoughts. One day while on the computer, a pop-up, "How to write a book", was relentless. My partner walked into the room and I said, "I think I'm going to write a book." The response was not what I expected and certainly not what I wanted. After a day of reflection and self-judgment, I realized that his words were mirroring what was in my unconscious mind.

Self-defeating words were very familiar to me; they lived in my mind. My mind, being a part of the Christ Mind, couldn't possibly be incompetent. This knowing would be my strength! My ambitious venture would require all my inner fortitude in challenging low-self-esteem, lack of self-trust, and ability. It would be necessary for me to step outside my comfort zone, no longer resist change, entertain other possibilities, and dare to do something different.

Did ego feel threatened by the idea of standing in power and taking ownership of my mind's creative energy? Was it threatened by stepping out of the belief that I was weak, vulnerable, powerless, and in a stagnate state? Was it fearful of rejection? That is the ego's game; it's the ego's world. This is the world that keeps sucking us back into itself.

I forgave my partner, myself (my mind),for believing that he was a body, I was a body and that it was all real. I asked the Holy Spirit, once again, to heal my mind and help me know we are all guiltless. None of this drama, book, bodies, or universe are real. It is only a dream! What is real, is Love!

# PROJECTION IN ACTION

I recall a situation that occurred a number of years ago; an example of unconscious projection involving my late husband. He offered to help with some renovations in an older home. When that morning arrived, he became extremely irritated. He tried to draw me into all kinds of arguments. Remaining neutral was difficult to maintain. It became clear to me this was not about a door, or anything else he attempted to create an argument about.

I finally asked him, "What is the real reason for your miserable-self?" I suggested perhaps he was resisting *what is* and wishing it were different. Rather than owning the conflict in his mind, he was busy trying to project that disharmony outside of himself. After thinking about it for a moment, he agreed indeed that was the real issue.

What we attempt to project outside of ourselves, is always only a problem inside our mind. In a situation when one feels inner discord, what appears to be an emotional resistance or reaction, it is because the act serves the ego mind, not the Higher Self.

# LOVE THY NEIGHBOUR AS THYSELF

*Love thy neighbour as thyself* - because your neighbour is really you. We are the imagined *others* in our lives. Regardless how situations present themselves in day to day relationships, it is important to try to see our image in others. The people we connect with most often bring us the greatest opportunities for healing. Whether it is with our immediate neighbours, or those within our work place, it doesn't matter; emotional pain is most transparent within close interactions.

Try to see beyond the mask of a body and attune to the emotional driver behind an intense situation. Most likely, you would find someone who is in great need of love and understanding; it may be you. Outward expressions of needs are difficult to observe initially within dramas. Emotional pain is projected onto others, in search for a bit of reprieve. Humanity is under a lot of stress; these stresses continually express themselves in the body as diseases.

Projection could cause a distraction and temporarily avoid facing one's greatest fears. The problem is firmly placed on others, boundaries and fences are created in an attempt to keep away the ugliness of family issues, and serious illnesses. It is only at that point, another human being may be able to reach out and greatly assist in healing the true sickness, which is in the mind.

Many layers of that onion would need to be peeled back to uncover the hidden emotional distress requiring healing. Certainly, anger would be the first emotion to address; then, perhaps fear, sadness, depression, rejection, and guilt.

So, what did my image in the mirror reveal to me? Disharmony, anger, hurt, sadness, rejection, and of course guilt. We are all the same, all a part of the same-sick mind. The mind just keeps recycling all that pain, trying to get rid of it, only to face it once again. It's a vicious circle.

# ONE MIND
# Fractured Mind
## Projections

SAME FACE
"OTHER"
NAMES
"OTHER"
MASKS

SEE
YOUR FACE
IN
"OTHERS"

FEAR

FEAR
Joe

Mary
PAIN

ANGER
Ray

GUILT
Jill

FEAR
ANGER
Bill
Joan
GUILT
Raymod

HATE
Marjorie
Ruth
GRIEF
Steven

Guilt
sell
FEAR
Albert
ANGER
Loyd
Jean
Rory

IDEA
HATE
Kathy
Jody
ANXIETY

PAIN
SAD
PAIN

ANGER
Duncan
HATE
Sam
GRIEF

LT PAIN
Vicky Bev
GUILT
Shirley
Ethel

Charlie

GRIEF
EA
ANXIETY
HATE

Joy
Eva
FEAR
Jake
Arthur

PAIN SADNESS
Warren

Toby

# THE BIG BANG

## SCAPEGOATS

The Bible story tells us that before we entered the fragmented or separated state, we were in the Garden of Eden - a place of perfection and peace. Adam and Eve were warned not to eat forbidden fruit from a tree. Apparently, Eve did what she was forbidden to do, which was take a bite out of an apple. Adam heard a voice, believed the words, and became frightened. This was the birth of the ego voice. As this story goes, Adam was told that they had *sinned*, and God was very angry. Immediately, they were filled with intense guilt for disobeying God. Adam blamed Eve. Eve blamed the snake and we have been frightened and guilty ever since. Everyone in our lives now serve as our scapegoats. This was the beginning of the projection and blame game. Does this story resemble another story?

In an act of religious symbolism, a priest conveyed the *sins* of the Israelites to a goat; it was sacrificed as penance for their sins, by being tossed off a cliff. People were no longer responsible for their actions because their sins were forgiven, they were someone else's (the goat's) problem.

Mayans were known to have their priests perform human sacrifices to cleanse them of their *sins*, so that the universe would give them a year of plenty. No need for anyone to take responsibility for their actions, unless you were the unfortunate one chosen to be sacrificed. What dumb luck!

We quite often blame the devil. The devil made me do it! Once again, I am not responsible for my actions, the devil is! The devil is really our ego voice, not out there but in our own mind. We need to be grateful for the devil, without the devil we may have to fess-up to our own messes! Of course, it is easier to simply blame the devil!

When it comes to projections, nothing is sacred, not even God. There are many devastations, for which we give full credit to God. Earthquakes, hurricanes, volcanoes, tornados, floods, and accidents are often called *acts of God*. Humanity cries, "Why did God let this happen? Why did God do this to us?" Perhaps still believing God was punishing humanity for eating that stupid apple.

What about (ego mind) humanity's responsibility? Building poorly constructed buildings, cities, and countries right on top of tectonic plates, in extremely vulnerable situations. Who is responsible for causing the earthquakes? Dams and water extractions, oil drilling (fracking), injection wells, as well as the construction of many extremely tall and heavy buildings, all contribute to destabilizing issues deep beneath the earth's surface.

Humanity's contribution to climate change is causing extreme weather across the world. All of us have personally witnessed, or heard of intense weather, down-pours of rain causing flooding, large hail, and devastating tornados. Irresponsible deforestation causing mud slides; drought giving rise to forest fires; snow falling in places that don't normally see snow. The polar ice cap is melting and oceans are rising. All of this having devastating consequences on bird and animal kingdom. Where is humanity's responsibility in this? Where is the ego mind that is the driver and creator of this mess?

Who is responsible for all the hate, terror, and human created pain and suffering? The world reflects what is going on within the mind. The mind continues to project inner disharmony outward in an attempt to get rid of it, simply refusing to take ownership and accountability.

I can go on and on about what is solely the responsibility of mankind (the mind). How arrogant of mankind to suggest that it is an act of God. This is clearly a personal and global projection. God supposedly is the problem. God is doing this to us. God is uncaring, willing to starve and kill his children because he is angry. If it wasn't for God doing all this to us, there would not be a problem. God is our scapegoat!

People can go to church and pay a priest to listen to their confessions; he says a few words, a declaration of God's forgiveness, tells them not to do that again. Affirmation of God's forgiveness is confirmed by ingesting a piece of bread and wine - symbolizing Jesus' flesh and blood; thus, sanctify their innocence. No responsibility is needed for the consequences of one's behavior. The mind firmly believes that God would have his own son sacrificed, killed for the *sins* of all his other children. Jesus is our scapegoat!

Scapegoat/projection has been going on for eons of time. Ceremonies of sacrificing - scapegoats, even when only symbolic, have been naturally accepted as normal, never questioning the seemingly lack of humanity's evolution - the presumed *civilized* world. Perhaps it is time to question many things.

The mind, through bodies, believing it is something that it is not, spends life over life, carrying the cross, for the initial thought of wanting to be special. Instead of facing made-up fear and comprehending the truth that none of it is real, the mind will continue to crucify itself by projecting guilt onto other parts of itself. What is certain, is that there is no-one else out there; it is one mind believing it is many. Other bodies are merely the one mind repetitively sacrificing parts of itself.

# CHAPTER

# 16

# WHO ARE WE?

*"As human beings, our greatness lies not so much in being able to remake the world - that is the myth of the atomic age, as in being able to remake ourselves."*

## MAHATMA GANDHI

It is a choice to re-enter into a life experience. Prior to the mind's awareness of entering into a body, intense discussions take place with a Council, Guides, and Soul-groups. Decisions are made based upon which lessons the fractured mind chooses to work on during this lifetime. There are choices regarding what kind of body, personality, family environment, and influences are needed to set the stage for this experience. Based on those decisions, personalities of the parents and siblings are also chosen, which would provide the appropriate experience to support a specific learning. The moment the personality is born into this illusionary world, it immediately enters into special relationships.

Agreements are made between separate minds to facilitate and provide a specific environment for the necessary foundation. This includes all outside beliefs and behaviors that could add to shape and form the personality of the newly entered body. All of which will become the focus of the separated mind's awareness.

All conditioning, incomplete experiences, influences brought forward from previous incarnations are also taken into consideration. This is an extremely intense process; infinite possibilities are entered into the planning. The mind's freedom of choice plays a big role. The exit time and circumstances during that situation are also established, taking into consideration all the possible variables that may exist. There may be as many as five probable exit opportunities.

Nothing is accidental, or a chance occurrence. There is no such thing as being at the wrong place at the wrong time. Everything happens at the precisely perfect time and place and is according to script. As devastating as the death of a loved one may be, it is what the mind planned to experience. All people and minds affected by that individual's death, also asked to have the resulting experience. These create opportunities for choices, which would facilitate the path of their soul's evolution. The intention is to learn, correct all false beliefs and progressively evolve the mind's thinking to be in-harmony with the Christ Mind - the True Self. The goal is to be able to see your face in others and recognize the face of Christ.

## THOUGHTS FEED EMOTIONAL PAIN

I'm sure we all noticed how thoughts are the drivers of our lives. That voice in the head that never seems to shut-up. It can be relentless, persistent, demanding attention, action, or retaliation; there is very little room for peace. Oh yes, there are moments in one's life when everything is joyful and worthy of experiencing. Enjoy it while it lasts because it is just a matter of time before all hell breaks loose again. It is the ego's world. It sucks you in; then, sits back and enjoys the drama. It's acting upon one's thoughts that get one into trouble. The deeply repressed guilt is continuously fueled and sustained by judgement and criticism of others. Keeping the projection of inner pain active makes this world go around in an endless cycle of not taking ownership of one's inner guilt.

All relationships play an equally big role, not only extremely intimate or significant relationships, but also seemingly insignificant ones. Relationships are all special in that they are predestined for a specific learning, with many opportunities for an intended outcome. All play unambiguous roles, assisting with deliberate lessons and consequential healing. Every experience is scripted into your life story to present ideal opportunities for the particular learning your soul requested.

Which voice is chosen for assistance in making decisions, will make a big difference. The mind either follows the advice of the ego, or advice of Spirit. One part of our mind, the ego side, is constantly projecting, so the world we believe we see is produced by ego. Thoughts are relentless, the voice that chatters obsessively over and over, sometimes called the monkey mind. Remember, the monkey would risk dying rather than letting go and learning a different way.

The Higher Self can try to get a word or image in edgewise only when there is a split-second lull in between thoughts. This communication is very subtle and could be easily missed or discounted. Usually only when our right-minded side is ready for something different, perhaps tired of what is, are subtle messages or images noticed.

## Is Seclusion the Answer?

*"Every experience, no matter how bad it seems, holds within it a blessing of some kind. The goal is to find it."*[1]

In a conversation with a friend, comments were made regarding the peaceful lives of Monks with their constant connection with God during frequent states of meditation and prayer. This particular life experience was divinely chosen for a purpose. Their praying and sitting in quiet repos contributes greatly to neutralizing negative energy in our world through a continuous projection of *Light* energy. For this we are grateful. All life experiences are chosen to serve a specific purpose in the mind.

One may question whether choosing to withdraw from relationships and daily human interactions is really conducive to spiritual growth. It is quite easy to be in the *now* without the daily issues of life. It's a challenge to be in a continuous state of peace and gratitude, when the weather, or insects play havoc with one's livelihood and the only source of sustenance for one's family. The experience of having to work every day, possibly under an extremely difficult boss or circumstances, brings about more anxiety than joy to the heart.

Dealing with different personalities of one's children and all the various problems that seem to present themselves sometimes minute by minute, could very easily leave one a bit depressed and desperate. Equally disconcerting is a situation where there may be a problem with addiction, either personally, or with loved ones. Mental, or physical health, and financial obligations could certainly put a damper on one's tranquil state in a hurry.

One seems to be tested every day within situations to choose differently. How we choose to react and handle personal relationships, how quickly and willingly we love and forgive others, determines the amount of potential Soul's growth. All experiences are divinely orchestrated, for an intended desired experience in a situation.

Mother Theresa lived among people on the street and was aware of their mental pain, while tending to their daily needs. The ability to understand the pain of humanity, which is our own, to be able to rise above, and reach other planes of awareness is so crucial in assisting with the evolution of the Soul. It is the day to day relationships that ultimately cause one to say, "Surely there must be another way." At this point, comes a desire for things to be different. Perhaps, too many intense dramas or a tragedy may catapult one into searching for answers, wanting a different experience without the constant fear, pain, and guilt looming over them.

Because of its awareness of being in a body, the mind has an opportunity to experience life from different perspectives, from which it can draw a tremendous amount of wisdom and understanding. So, don't withdraw and hide from human interactions and relationships because you will lose an opportunity for tremendous spiritual growth.

Our ingrained ego personality is not easily overcome. Even when we spend time meditating, centering ourselves, and even set intention upon intention to be more tolerant, loving, and patient we are shocked to see how easy it is to get tripped up.

I have a sister who's *Soul's* purpose is to continually test me. After spending time with her, I always reflect upon the truth that she was placed in my life to teach and test my patience. Sometimes just as I start to think that I have, at last, managed to keep my cool and direct only love and kindness towards her, as I addressed her daily needs, she manages to do it again! She will always keep me humble. I look forward to one day passing the test, only then, I will believe that I have a remote chance of being truly enlightened. I love my sister dearly!

This brings to mind an Indian anecdote *Deepak Chopra* mentions in his book, *How to Know God.*

*The ascetic goes to the mountaintop to become enlightened. He fasts and prays constantly; he gives up all worldly desires in favor of meditation. His renunciation goes on for many years until the day when he realizes he has finally arrived. No matter where he looks, he senses only the unbounded bliss of pure awareness without attachment of any kind. Overjoyed, he rushes down into the village below to tell everyone and as he is going along he runs into a crowd of drunken revelers. Quietly he tries to thread his way through, but one drunk after another bumps him and makes a crude remark. Finally, the ascetic can't stand it and cries, "Get out of my way!" At that instant he stops, turns around, and goes back to the mountain.*

# CHAPTER

# 17

# SPECIALNESS

*"But what is different calls for judgement, and this must come from someone "better," someone incapable of being like what he condemns, "above" it, sinless by comparison with it. And thus does specialness become a means and end at once. For specialness not only sets apart, but serves as grounds from which attack on those who seem "beneath" the special one is "natural" and "just". The special ones feel weak and frail because of differences, for what would make them special is their enemy."*

ACIM[1]

Specialness, one judging another in order to rise above the other, whether observed in people, or countries, is the primary cause of a tremendous amount of disharmony, attacks, and wars. There is constant manoeuvring and juggling for the position of being better, more influential, worthier, stronger, smarter, more fearful, or different, reinforcing the belief that they are the most special. Only one thing, person, or country can be in that position; it is not possible for two to be - the *most* special one.

One's life becomes imprisoned by this need for specialness. It is a constant battle to hold on to the crown one places upon one's head. It appears to be a very important tool of the ego and the driver of this illusionary world. The sick mind initially made its decision to separate wanting to be the special one. It has spent lifetimes using its specialness to fragment itself further. Needing to be unique, prettier, uglier, sicker, victimized, victimizer, smarter, challenged (physically or mentally), and any other superlative one can use to stand out and be noticed.

Specialness demands that there is anger, conflict, and an enemy. Judgement follows to set those parameters in place. There must be a source of comparison. To grade specialness, one needs to be less than someone else, this extends to groups, and countries. This is the hypocrisy of ego's thinking of setting boundaries. Where there is self-love and love of all, there are no boundaries, there's simply a continuous flow, one into the other.

## IS SPECIAL TREATMENT LOVING?

Valentine's Day is intended to be a day to honor and show our love to the *special* people in our lives. This day certainly holds the trade mark of the ego. On this day, one's love is expected to be expressed mostly through materialistic expectations, strongly encouraged by commercially driven spending.

On this day, there is a clear distinction between those who have love and romance in their lives with an appearance of specialness, and those who do not experience love and never felt special in any way. For them, this day sustains a different kind of specialness, one of victimhood, a fully realized and embodiment of self-hatred. Both groups are the same, both lack self-love and demand it from others, even if it is in the form of pity. Both kinds of *specialness* are equally fulfilled. Being different, not the same, sets people apart, which in turn only serves to make one, or the other special.

We nurture specialness in our children, by constantly reinforcing a necessity to be: the prettiest, handsomest, tallest, fastest, smartest, or most gifted. We repeatedly compare them to others, which encourages competition. When we tell our children they are special, we do not realize the negative impact we may be creating on their psyche, their relationships with others, and society as a whole.

We all have noticed children out in shopping malls, or public places reacting in a loud demanding manner, having a temper tantrum, constantly seeking attention, acknowledgement, and wanting to be noticed. Behavioral problems in schools create havoc in a learning environment, with children competing for positions of specialness. As they get older and are no longer treated with the same degree of attention, there is a festering of problems. There may be difficulty in establishing a healthy assimilation into society.

Perhaps society needs to bear most of the responsibility for lack of family interactions at home. The world places materialistic demands with its consequent allure on society, closely followed by a financial debt, which are often the drivers behind requiring both parents to go to work to pay bills. The child rearing responsibility is passed onto others to discipline, guide, and love them.

Guilt plays a big role on parents who ultimately lavish their children with gifts to make up for lack of their time and love; children come to associate materialistic things with love. Lack of parental supervision allows children to go off seeking to fulfill their needs of attention elsewhere, opening the potential to abusive behavior both to themselves and others.

The ego's goal is to set one apart by constantly comparing and competing. Children learn how to gain attention very early in life. Unfortunately, when there is a sense of lack, which is not adequately fulfilled by others, one resorts to denial, deceit, judgment, criticism, and actively projecting blame onto others. There is no limit to what action may be taken in order to gain what is believed lacking. To get the much-needed attention, certain skills are learned, causing one to become a proficient liar and actor. It can become so problematic that it is difficult to distinguish the truth from falsehood.

This explains a lot of humanity's behavior. Many of the mass shootings in churches and schools may be driven by those who demand to be different, stand apart from others and noticed. Their need for attention has no boundaries. Many extreme behaviors have their base desired outcomes driven by a need of being special. The ego demands to be noticed, different, and separate from others; its life depends on it.

Children's innocence and trust prevents them from questioning behavior of those within the family group or society. They eagerly watch and learn by examples in day to day interactions. What is dearly lacking is an understanding of self-love, self-healing, or the need to take responsibility for one's thinking and beliefs. There is limited awareness, regarding how these influence and ultimately create one's life's experiences.

It is the ego's intention to continue to fragment and separate. Only a few are chosen to be special, envied, and placed above all others to create a noticeable difference of status. A clear distinction in values and prominence supports and nurtures an obvious setting apart and firmly establishes separation. How many people idolize movie actors, the royal family, the rich, and famous. This type of worship does tremendous damage to the mind's self-esteem and feelings of self-worth. The idea of being equally as important and valuable as everybody else, is too unbelievable to fathom. The ego is an unscrupulous force to be reckoned with.

## SPECIAL RELATIONSHIPS

*"When another person's welfare means more to you than your own, when even his or her life means more to you then your own, only then can you say you love. Anything else is just business, give and take."*[2]

True love does not hesitate to lay down one's life for another. We've come to believe that love and hate can co-exist, conveniently switch from one to the other when necessary, in order to gain what we believe is lacking, as we search for happiness. In our relationships, we seek to find someone to *complete* us. When we feel that they no longer provide us with support, love, or foster our self-worth, we punish by denying them love. We easily slip into projecting blame onto others, insisting they are the cause of our unhappiness.

Our relationships always have conditions. You fulfill your part of the unconscious contract in providing me with what I need to feel special, and I will do the same for you. This could be in the form of gifts, power, love, time, money, status, favors, emotional, and/or financial support. What we believe we lack in ourselves, we look for someone else to provide for us. These would complete us, somehow make us whole.

We negotiate with power, each giving our power away in order to be special. There also may be a conscious taking of power from the other if what one wants is not given willingly. You give to me, I give to you. If you no longer hold up your unconscious part of the bargain, there may be an abuse of each other, or oneself, or the relationship may simply be dissolved. All things of love, including never harming anyone, is a choice. Love is a way of being; it is constant and can never turn into hate.

To experience love, one must give it generously and willingly with no conditions. It is important to love oneself completely, not in an egotistic way, but by acknowledging and honoring one's True Reality. It is impossible to measure Love; it is limitless and the source of immense happiness and peace.

The few that decide to work together to find a solution, are able to tap into an opportunity of tremendous potential for incredible spiritual growth. It is one fractured mind assisting another fractured mind, working together to find their way back to True Reality, the whole Christ Mind. The mind is dreaming a dream within which it is experiencing itself through multiplicity in order to awaken from this dream to find itself safe at Home.

# CHAPTER
# 18

# WILL ANYTHING
# FILL THAT VOID?

*"No one who comes here, but must still have hope, some lingering illusion, or some dream that there is something outside of himself that will bring happiness and peace to him. If everything is in him this cannot be so.......... This is the purpose he bestows upon the body; that it seek for what he lacks, and give him what would make himself complete. And thus, he wanders aimlessly about, in search of something that he cannot find, believing that he is what he is not."*

ACIM [1]

Who can say they are truly fulfilled and blissfully happy? I don't believe it is possible in this world. What one seeks is not material things, but parts of Self (Mind) that have been fragmented and projected out.

It is like *Humpty Dumpty* knowing something is terribly wrong, but unable to figure out what it could be. He sees the brokenness and fractured pieces in complete disarray, but even though his life depends on it, he cannot figure out what is wrong with the picture, or how to fix it. He has no idea how to glue himself back together again. With passage of time, he has gotten used to being broken, accepting the situation as normal. He simply chooses to overlook the continual pain, fear, and guilt.

The mind has forgotten it was once whole and now appears to be broken. It made a bad decision and like *Humpty Dumpty* seems unaware of a solution. Something is lacking, but what? What is lacking is the desire to understand the cause of the seemingly brokenness, emptiness, and nothingness of this world. By simply accepting the condition as normal, we lack the motivation to do anything to change it.

We spend so much time dreaming, desiring, and purchasing things. For awhile our new things appear to make us happy. Nevertheless, it isn't long until once again, we are unconsciously driven to search for something else, perhaps new shoes, a trip, a new home, or a new relationship. The search is endless. Throughout our life's journey, we are eternally trying to fill that void. The ego keeps sucking us into this world with materialistic things with which to fill that void. It doesn't have any intention of directing us to what it is that we greatly miss and dearly lack, knowing full well we could never find it in this world.

Perhaps food can fill that void within us. The greatest threat right now to the mind and by extension the physical body, is obesity. What has been accepted as a normal body weight continues to change and now, more than ever before, human beings are becoming increasingly larger. In response to this health crisis, there is an equal explosion of weight loss diets, exercise programs and magic pills. The problem is not in the body, the body is merely a symbol of guilt. Of course, now added to the existing layers of guilt, is the additional burden of feeling a loss of self-control when one has overeaten. This layering of guilt can go on several times a day, burying it deeper into the illusion.

Our continuation of projecting our guilt outward onto others causes more fragmentation, resulting in a tremendous amount of bodies that need to be fed. The world's population is increasing by leaps and bounds, food supply is greatly taxed, causing a concern that it won't be long before there is a vast shortage. There is an increased drive to produce food faster and in higher quantities.

Grains, fruits, and vegetables frequently have their genetic makeup altered to increase production and resistance to diseases and insects. Fruits and vegetables are picked before they are fully ripe and sprayed with chemicals to be shipped distances to markets. No wonder they are tasting more and more like card-board, and their shelf-life is short lived. Consequently, a lot of food is spoiled and wasted.

Animals are fed genetically modified grains, which are mixed with hormones to increase their growth; thus, reducing the time it takes to get meat to consumer. It takes approximately 36 days from hatching, for a baby chick to go to market. We are eating bloated obese baby chicks; nutritional value and taste are dearly lacking.

Like in much of the food produced for human consumption, the flavour of the final product leaves a lot to be desired. You may have noticed that most of your food has been injected with *natural flavourings*, probably because nothing seems appealing to our senses, especially our taste sense. Most importantly, though, the more appealing a product seems to our mind, the more we will crave and consume.

You may be surprised to learn that natural flavourings and what we believe to be natural, are not very natural at all. There can be as many as 2200 combinations of chemicals that contribute to the make-up of natural flavorings. Our lack of *comfort* in our body and a feeling of well-being, drives us to try to find it in food, or other means of immediate gratification.

In his book *The Dorito Effect, Mark Schatzker* explains the journey of flavourings and spices that are added to our food, how the process was fine tuned and led to the refined desired outcome of the final product. The product that you cannot eat enough of! The chosen formula for *natural flavorings* used in most of all the food we eat today, is decided by how much they attribute to an *effect in the mind*; the flavors that create a feeling of *contentment* and *happiness* in the *mind.*

How many of you have craved your childhood favorite food, lovingly created and served by a loved one? Could it be that the taste of the food is greatly enhanced by a lingering memory of loving energy that surrounded it? The desired comfort is found in a combination of fulfilling our need for love and the awareness of pleasure and happiness provided by the interpretation of the many senses within the mind. That is the recipe for the ultimate natural flavourings that are injected into most foods we ingest in order to fill that happiness void.

What the mind is so desiring, needing, and lacking is *happiness*. This is the all too constant *need state*. The need is incessantly increased. Like all other addictions, the consumer needs more to receive the same gratification, which can never truly fill that void. This is the driver behind all materialist desires in this world.

So, like an obese baby chick, we, the bodies, are also getting obese younger because the mind is dearly lacking happiness and is driven to fill that void within each one of us with addictive products or behaviors.

The mind keeps projecting more and more comfort food into a body attempting to create permanent happiness and contentment. It's a drive toward recapturing a memory of a natural and perpetual state of one's True Self. No amount of food will bring the state of comfort that the mind craves. No amount of so called *natural* flavourings, food, trips, material things, lovers, or money will ever fill that *happiness* void.

What will it take for humanity to desire a solution to the endless problem of a void that can never be filled by anything in this world? What is necessary before one seeks solutions which are out of this world? The ego's solution is to repetitively project and recycle the pain within the mind. A realization of our True Reality is the only thing that would give us unimaginable bliss and happiness.

Society is obsessed with *selfies*. Humanity loves taking pictures of the body, if only, just only, one could see one's True Self. If human eyes could see, they would not be able to fully grasp the profound beauty of the True Self.

*"The world you see is the delusional system of those made mad by guilt. Look carefully at this world, and you will realize that this is so. For this world is the symbol of punishment, and all the laws that seem to govern it are the laws of death. Children are born into pain and in pain. Their growth is attended by suffering, and they learn of sorrow and separation and death. Their minds seem to be trapped in their brain, and its powers to decline if their bodies are hurt. They seem to love, yet they desert and are deserted. They appear to lose what they love, perhaps the most insane belief of all. And their bodies wither and gasp and are laid in the ground, and are no more."*[2]

The mind, as a body, agonizes over daily decisions and worries endlessly about whether it is the right decision or not. It believes the body can fret, scheme, and worry over minute details to determine a future outcome. The mind believes it is at the mercy of the body's choices and blames it for every wrong decision and deed. Holding the body responsible and believing it has any control over anything, is insane. It is akin to blaming the avatar in a video game for a wrong decision, rather than blaming the controller who is making and implementing the choices.

The ego mind does what it must to prolong life in a body. It may subject a body to procedures such as plasma infusions to slow aging. A California company was the developer of this process which was made available in other states[3]. During this process, plasma extracted from 16 to 25-year-old bodies is introduced into veins of older clients to rejuvenate sluggish, shrinking cells. The cost of this 2-hour procedure could be more than $10,000, but claims to extend life to 150 years and beyond.

When a body dies, the mind may choose to have it preserved in a solution or frozen to be brought back to life in the future, hoping it would live forever. Many bodies are buried with all their jewelry, in beautiful and comfortable caskets in the ground, waiting to rise from the grave at the second coming of Christ. The mind, as a body, often gazes up to the sky hoping to see Christ coming down to save them both.

The great news is that the body can do nothing. Therefore, the body is not responsible for any *sins*. A thought does not leave its source, the mind that creates it. There is an innate desire to heal the initial guilt; the original fragmentation of the Self. Mind yearns to draw all the fragmented pieces back to itself, so it can wake up from this nightmare. It simply does not know how to make this happen.

## CONNECTING WITH ONE'S INNER LIGHT

*"I will there be light. Let me behold the light that reflects God's Will and mine."*[4]

One night, while stirring in my sleep, I sensed a bright light. Opening the body's eyes, revealed being completely immersed in a brilliant light extending beyond and filling all space. Immediately thinking, "What on earth! Where is it coming from? Is someone in the house or backyard?"

Still blindingly bright, the light began to withdraw. "Did my daughter decide to come home, even though she planned on staying at a friend's place after work?" The light withdrew some more. Starting to feel worried, I checked the time, it was 2:20 a.m., "That's late to be coming home from work, she's usually home by midnight." The light receded further, now revealing the bedroom wall with the closed door, but still streaming intensely above and through any and all openings.

Becoming worried, "There must be a problem!" The light continued to retreat, revealing the ceiling of the bedroom. Now beginning to panic, "I'd better go and see what's wrong." The light very quickly receded and dimmed; then, with an audible "Click", the light was out!

I got out of bed to investigate. My daughter's shoes were not by the door. There was no light in her bedroom. She did not come home. Completely perplexed, I looked out the back window, only seeing the darkness of the night. "Where did the light come from and where did it go?"

The *Light* was mine. The *Light* didn't go anywhere. The very second, I was aware of *seeing through a body's eyes and thoughts of worry, anxiety and fear entered the mind*, the *Light* progressively became obscured. An illusion began to appear and my *Light* disappeared. It's *fear* and all *negative thoughts* that are not in-harmony with the *Light* that create our illusionary world and keep us imprisoned within it.

How do we reconnect with our *Light*? We need to stop getting sucked into the daily drama, change our thoughts, and belief systems. The body, made of guilt, having layers of additional guilt placed upon it, covers the Truth of Reality and keeps the *Light* firmly hidden away.

The knowledge of your *True Essence*, the *Holy Son of God - Pure Love, Pure Light,* has never left the mind. It is the same *Love* that is within every fractured mind, a gift which is extended, or projected onto others; then, mirrored back to self. Clearing our vision and seeing the *Light* in others is the answer to awakening from this dream. It is our *Light*, mirrored back to us.

*"Man has to be saved from the saviours of mankind! The religious people - they kidded themselves and fooled the whole of mankind."*[5]

The initial response to the fact that *Jesus* dictated *A Course in Miracles* may cause some to roll their eyes in disbelief. It is hard to understand such communication would occur in this supposedly advanced and seemingly evolved civilization. The Bible and its testaments of spiritual communications written more than 500 years after the fact, are accepted as truth. Those teachings have had an intense hold on humanity for over 2000 years with far fewer questions about their authenticity. Humans have chosen blind faith and killed in its honor, without questioning the validity of that belief, or righteousness of that action.

How can war or violence be in line with teachings of Jesus, or the will of a loving and caring Creator, no matter what religious disguise ego takes? Now would be an appropriate time for Spirit communication within this broken and troubled world. We certainly could use a savior right now, to offer guidance, wisdom, or tools with which the mind can save itself from more lifetimes of misery.

My wakeup call was a dream letting me know Jesus would be my guide Home, through a book called *A Course in Miracles*. These new teachings turn the accepted knowledge of organized religion upside down. For eons we have been taught there is only one way to save humanity. It is tremendously comforting in knowing Jesus is driving my car and will continue to sustain me on this path. That is my right mind's choice. What do you choose? Stand in your power, arm yourself with information and wisdom, and don't simply follow the sheep to the slaughter. Choose again!

## AWARENESS OF BEING PART OF ONE MIND

*"The Body's serial adventure, from the time of birth to dying are the theme of every dream the world has ever had. The "hero" of this dream will never change, nor will its purpose. Though the dream itself takes many forms and seems to show a great variety of places and events wherein its "hero" finds itself, the dream has but one purpose, taught in many ways. This single lesson does it try to teach again, and still again, and yet once more; that it is cause and not effect. And you*

*are its effect, and cannot be its cause. Thus are you not the dreamer, but the dream. And so you wander idly in and out of places and events that it contrives. That this is all the body does is true, for it is but a figure in a dream."* [6]

The real breakthrough comes when we start to identify ourselves with the mind, rather than a body with a name. We are the mind, whose awareness is in a body having a life experience. It is the same, as when we are imagining a scene, a past, or future event in our heads. It is really the mind imagining that it is a body, having these thoughts.

Nothing leaves its source. The people within the scenes in one's night-time dream cannot leave the dreamer's mind, or somehow enter from outside the dreamer's mind. They remain within, part of the mind, and are *only* in the mind. Day-time dreams are no different; the mind simply believes that as a body, it is interacting and communicating with other living people. They are all just figments of the mind's imagination.

All bodies in both dreams are merely representative or symbolic of many unhealed issues. Both night and day dreams represent the fear, sadness, anger, guilt, lack of love, and self-esteem within the mind. These issues are projected out onto forms of bodies because the ego mind refuses to accept responsibility for them. Both dreams mirror these issues back to notice, acknowledge, embrace, heal, or celebrate. The mind is delusional; it is, in essence, fracturing itself into many parts, simply to avoid owning the part it played in causing its mental issues. Each time your mind heals one of these issues, or makes a correction, it loosens the chains that bind it to this dream world, or the wall full of shadows.

The mind's tremendous inner pain is frequently expressed in the world. The earth explodes and cracks, trees and animals are diseased and becoming extinct, the sky reacts violently, and oceans churn furiously. In all this terror and drama it is extremely difficult to remain neutral and not be repetitively sucked into this illusion. It is becoming obvious that the world is unremittingly reflecting global extreme inner guilt.

What is becoming obvious is an overwhelming sense that humanity is getting increasingly tired of the status quo and desires another way. The end is certain; all the fractured pieces of the mind will eventually be healed and awakened to oneness. It is just a matter of time. One can only speculate how many more life experiences it will take to accomplish this awakening.

Continual references to the fact that the *I* is really a fractured piece of the mind that is delusional, centers my awareness and objectivity. The intent is to have an overview of the drama while remaining neutral as an observer, rather than an active participant. It is a lifelong process with intention and determination to wake up. One must remain vigilant and continue processing *forgiveness* through the *Holy Spirit*. Sooner or later there will be clarity. Patience is a virtue that is well worth the wait.

*"Father, I did not make myself, although in my insanity I thought I did. Yet as Your Thought, I have not left my Source, remaining part of Who created me. Your son, my Father, calls on You today. Let me remember You created me. Let me remember my Identity. And let my sinlessness arise again before Christ's vision, through which I would look upon my brothers and myself today."*[7]

Our *true identity* lies within the Christ Mind, which is a creation of God's Thought. Do not mistaken the above quote to be referencing to your *illusionary-self*, your human body. The mind thought it created itself within a body, and in so doing, left the Source. It is a call for Truth to prevail within a sick mind; thoughts do not leave their source. We must understand that our True Reality is still in God's Thought, where the Christ Mind resides, an extension of God's Mind, the Source.

# CHAPTER
# 19

# HOW DOES DISEASE
# MANIFEST?

*"The guiltless mind cannot suffer. Being sane, the mind heals the body because it has been healed. The sane mind cannot conceive of illness because it cannot conceive of attacking anyone or anything. I said before that illness is a form of magic. It might be better to say that it is a form of magical solution."*

## ACIM[1]

During one of my written meditations, I asked my Guides to help me understand: "If a body is simply a thought in a separated mind; then, how does disease manifest in an imagined body?"

This was the response:

*It is a projection of the sick mind; ego's answer to the guilt accrued by a belief that separation from the creator was real. The creative energy of the separated mind slows down in vibration tremendously when its belief system and thoughts are that of the ego - one of guilt.*

*The image of the illusionary body is a creation of condensed energy. Thought is energy in motion, creating heavy low energy infractions. Emotional heavy energy is stagnating, festering and moving within a limited space. When a thought is not in line or in sync with the limitless expansions of the true one Mind, the deeper the mind sinks into the illusionary thought (ego) system, the more limited it becomes.*

*Spirit creation is expansion without limitation. Disease or sickness is projected from the mind into a body. Sickness limits and condenses into an "imprisoned like" state, still constantly moving and still creating within a more confined space. Like a car stuck trying to take off, but unable to go anywhere. The creativity of the mind is stagnated, stuck. Not being in line with its True Self, it creates and accumulates stagnate creative energy.*

*All this energy is reflective of negative thoughts carried forward. Eventually, this energy needs to use the body's energy to expand; it expands beyond its borders into the body until it chokes itself because it's no longer sustained by its own negative energy. The body dies. The Spirit is reborn, or projected out again into another body with another opportunity to correct and align the "thoughts" with the reality of the mind's True Self.*

## WHAT IS A BODY?

**"The body is a fence the Son of God imagines he has built, to separate parts of his Self from other parts. It is within this fence he thinks he lives, to die as it decays and crumbles. For within this fence he thinks that he is safe from love"**[2]

The body was created as a scapegoat, a symbol of the projected initial guilt felt at the moment of having the original thought of separating from God. The body now housed all fear, pain, and guilt. This was a convenient solution to rid the mind of intense pain of guilt and fear of God's imaginary retribution.

The mind assumed awareness of all experiences through a body, believing it was now a body. The mind immediately removed all reminders of the part it played in the separation scenario and started to project guilt unto other parts of itself. This triggered the *big bang* fragmentation, separating the mind into many parts. It was a way to try to escape taking accountability for the initial thought. Well, it's not working; the mind's guilt did not go away. The desire to escape this thought continues to go horribly wrong.

A body is simply an imagined thought in the mind, as with all thoughts when fed by more of the same thoughts, they take on a life of their own. The initial thought in the mind was no different. A world was created by a turbulence of emotional upheaval within the mind's mistaken belief of the reality of a thought; a thought manifested into form. The mind now believes the body and the universe are real. Therein lies the problem!

All thoughts are made of energy, including a body within that thought. Negative energy is denser than positive energy and moves much slower. The body, created by a negative thought, is a pocket of concentrated, slow moving energy. Imagine the body as a pocket of dense energy contained within a mesh bag. The holes or spaces of the mesh bag allow continuously moving light energy to easily pass through. Positive thoughts composed of lighter energy are able to flow freely though the body, a pocket of slow-moving energy.

Since most thoughts and beliefs within the mind are negative, slow moving energy, this adds to the difficultly of passing through an already dense body. Pieces of the slower energy get snagged. When thoughts are changed to positive, those pieces loosen and pass through more easily, possibly creating only a hic-up, or a head-ache within the awareness of the body.

The thoughts that are contained in our minds, live as informational energy in every cell of our bodies. It is a highway of communication from the mind, as it sends a flow of information and intelligence in and out, throughout the whole body. That same information; then, streams through the body, feeding, sustaining, and creating good or bad health.

All beliefs incessantly entangled with poisonous, destructive thoughts create blocks for any clear flowing, lighter energy. When there is a pattern of negative thoughts, beliefs and behaviors, energy pockets continue to become denser, build upon themselves and grow larger becoming energy blocks constrained within a prison-like space. If negative thinking and beliefs continue, original pockets of energy blocks may not remain in a specific part of the body; they may expand to other areas of the body as well.

This continuation of negative behavior now becomes toxic to the body. When years of toxicity are added to the formula, the conclusion is not good.

If none of those energy impulses are altered by changing the psychological structure within the mind, there is a very real possibility that the contained negatively fed energy will morph into more serious health issues.

Energy is always moving, always wanting to change, always creating. If it is contained within a limited space for awhile, it will break-through and expand beyond its borders ultimately consuming the body.

## THOUGHTS ARE CREATIVE

Everyone is aware of uninterrupted and somewhat obsessive thoughts that stream throughout our minds, everyday, all day, and sometimes even relentlessly throughout the night. Sleep can be elusive, especially when there are increased stresses and worries in one's life. We could have as many as 80,000 thoughts everyday and 95% of those thoughts are the same thoughts that are in our minds every day. An interesting article in *How Psychology Combats false and Self-Limiting Beliefs,* [3] references are made to our many thoughts and limiting beliefs becoming damaging to our bodies.

Relentless, repetitive thoughts are extremely creative. Positive thoughts create light energetic creations; however, most frequent creations are connected to negative intentions, purposefully, in order to keep the mind distracted and entangled with them, feeding the illusion. There are some pleasant thoughts, but most thoughts lead to stress and suffering. There is always a problem that requires solutions. The ego mind persistently needs attention, praise, admiration, acceptance, control, power, and money.

These thoughts often have an emotional component added onto them, triggering anger, hate, guilt, and blaming someone else for the cause of all problems. All of them carry a great deal of urgency and importance to be dealt with immediately. One can get so drawn into looking for solutions, it is difficult to break free from the thoughts, causing a tremendous amount of stress and often depression.

If one is constantly depressed or pessimistic, situations and people of the same energetic quality will appear in one's life. If one has a sunny disposition, always seeing the glass half full, people and circumstances drawn to one's life will reflect a positive outlook on life. Many opportunities and a much happier life will unfold for those who look at the world through rose colored glasses. Negative energy will do its best to repel positive energy;

however, because positive energy is lighter, it easily infiltrates heavier negative energy, causing it to disintegrate. It is important to maintain positive thoughts and behaviors if one wishes to maintain the health of the mind and body.

## HOW ARE EMOTIONS DRIVEN BY THOUGHTS?

*"The enemy is fear. We think it is hate but, it is fear."*[4]

Fear is the most powerful of all the negative emotions. Fear attracts more fear and could have paralyzing effects on the mind. It has the possibility of not only being destructive to oneself, but also harmful to others. One person's reaction to fear could propel masses of people into a fear-based frenzy, having potentially devastating results. There is no need to be fearful when you attune your thoughts, beliefs, and behaviors to positive energy. Fear is a heavy, dark energy and cannot survive in positive or Light energy. Continuously swaying one's thoughts from one extreme to another, good to bad and back again, leads to disturbing results creating an immense amount of suffering. Both forces will repeatedly be drawn to you, becoming entangled in a battle for control.

Thoughts are relentless. All thoughts of past mistreatments, verbal and physical abuse, as well as unresolved emotional and psychological issues can be incisively turbulent within the mind, rehashing, replaying conversations, and situations over and over. Frequently reliving and reaffirming painful emotions give them continuous life. Thoughts of desiring to retaliate, wanting others to feel the same pain, recreates the situation in the mind as real as though it happened yesterday. The distress it causes, along with the damage it creates in a mind and body, is monumental.

The children's nursery rhyme, *sticks and stones may break your bones, but words can never hurt you* is only partially true. Words can certainly hurt the mind when one takes them seriously and will eventually kill the body. Health is affected by name-calling, whether inflicted upon oneself, by others, or abuse of someone else. Self-punishment or any verbal abuse leaves a devastating energy block in the body.

Frequently running people down along with repetitive self-criticism causes damaging results. It is an already sick mind made sicker. Words like:

"What a stupid thing I've done; I am dumb, fat, and ugly; I can't do it, this is impossible; I am a horrible person and completely unlovable; You are useless and will never amount to anything; I wish you'd die; I never wanted you." Whether it is said only once, or often, it becomes real. By choosing to accept it to be true, you give it power, give it life. Even just spending a minimal amount of time thinking it might be true, would become demoralizing to the mind triggering energy pockets within the body.

If your workplace is a source of stress, perhaps a co-worker or boss is frequently belittling you and making life miserable, it may be tempting to keep those infractions alive in your mind, reliving them with your hourly thoughts. When you do so; however, you are setting yourself up for repetitive situations. Similar situations continue to be recreated in your everyday world. The world you see will mirror that same misery back to you. If you change jobs, but don't change your thoughts, you will probably find the same situation facing you again. Back again with the same obsessive negative thoughts, now added to the previous one, the stage is now set for a health crisis.

Stress initially affects the skin, the largest organ of the body; rashes may begin to break out. People who are more susceptible to colds, the flu, yeast infections, or skin rashes are those who are psychologically and emotionally stressed. Prolonged negative behavior could potentially lead to major energy blocks, as energy attempting to pass through the body gets jammed inside. A flow of negative energy stemming from anxiety and worry may begin to appear as immune deficiency disorders.

Most accidents can be attributed to the increased pace of society and our need for immediate emotional fulfilment. The focus on materialistic values with a drive to attain more things for self-gratification creates negative energy, which is nervous, careless, distracted, and most times angry. Accidents are outside forces slowing us down and forcing us to take time to reassess our priorities and values. The paths, we have been on, need a directional change.

## UNFINISHED BUSINESS IS HEAVY BAGGAGE

I would often ask residents in a nursing home, this question, "If you could go back in time to a stressful situation, for which you somehow felt responsible, with the accumulated knowledge you have today, would you have done things differently?" Without hesitation they'd reply, "Yes."

They are encouraged to forgive themselves because they did what they thought was best, based on what they knew at that time; they simply did not know any better. Also, they need to be forgiving towards anyone else who was part of that scene because, they too, did the best they knew how at the time. Assistance is given in releasing any residual negative emotions, along with encouragement to embrace the learning instead. This is a process anyone could use to help activate healing at anytime.

This method of healing and forgiveness is better than none at all. Until one is able to grasp a truth that this world is an illusion, nothing was done to oneself or others and all are guiltless, any form of forgiveness is good. It is through this manner of healing that the mind moves closer to awakening from this dream.

Unfinished business is most noticeable when a body is approaching death. In a *No One Dies Alone* program, while sitting with a resident, one of two states is often observed. As the mind's awareness of the body is in the process of being withdrawn, the body may be in a state of comfort and peace, just waiting for a timely shutting down of its organs, or in an obvious state of restlessness, uneasiness, and clearly not ready for transition. Even though they are no longer able to communicate, it is important to remind their minds of their True Reality.

Guidance is provided for healing all emotional wounds, while activating the forgiveness process. They are reminded of loved ones being there to greet them, as they enter a place of wondrous beauty. As well as being assured there is absolutely nothing to fear and to know emphatically that they are dearly loved. The body, then, enters a more peaceful state and when the mind is ready, its awareness is removed. This information is familiar to the mind; it was simply repressed, depressed, and seemingly forgotten.

Sickness is a big distraction, placing the mind's focus on the body and fear of death, drawing it into a crises and further into the illusion. Odds are in the ego's favor; the result will be the death of a body, not the death of ego, or the illusion. One's personality continues beyond death, a choice will be made to return, to have another try at moving beyond, forward, and toward one's eventual awakening.

A big step toward healing the mind is loving yourself, loving others even when you really don't feel like it and began a process of reprogramming your mind. Never withhold love! Do loving things without any conditions, self accolades, or expecting anything in return. If you do a loving thing and tell someone about it, you are doing it for your ego's need to be liked, respected, and honored. Don't feed your ego, don't give it life. Free your Spirit instead and work towards ending this birth and death cycle.

# CHAPTER
# 20

# DOES SICKNESS SERVE
# A PURPOSE?

*"The pain you feel are messengers.*
*Listen to them".*

## Rumi

My family lived on a farm in a rural area of Manitoba, Canada. At that time, the Sears and Eaton's catalogues were the only source for obtaining things not grown, or raised on the farm. There were some grocery and hardware stores in a nearby hamlet of Pine River, but they couldn't hold a candle to the merchandise available through the catalogues.

Every November, my mother would spend time choosing items for her catalogue purchases. Among other things, most items were to serve as Christmas gifts. As a child, I remember sitting beside my mother, wide eyed and excited by all the beautiful, different things available in the catalogues. There were several pages full of chocolates and candy. My mother chose one of the boxes of chocolates, as part of her order, which made me squeal with delight. I asked, "Are the chocolates for me?" My mother said, "No, they are for your sister." My older sister was always a sickly child, and our mother always treated her differently. When I asked my mother, "Why not for me too?" She replied, "Because you are healthy, and your sister is sick."

At this crucial point in my life, my four-year-old mind understood that to be loved and feel special, I needed to be sick.

I often suffered from frequent chest colds accompanied by a horrible cough. My child's mind clearly noticed that my mother did little to attend to my needs, my father would try to comfort and nurse me back to health. My mother instead would *appear* to be very impatient and annoyed with me. Around the age of ten, I experienced intense abdominal pain; it was my father who noticed there was a problem, expressed concern, and addressed the issue. An appendectomy was needed because of a very inflamed appendix.

An inability to process a perceived lack of love and emotional support caused an energy blockage, which festered and became a very real health crisis. My decision to attain love and attention from my mother through sickness, backfired. Unfortunately, my unconscious mind did not let go of that strategy.

## HEALING WITHIN A SPECIAL RELATIONSHIP

During my married life as in most marriages, many personal issues were brought into the union. Much like everyone else in this world, my husband had his own problems with self-worth, self-love, and self-confidence. He was very much an introvert, trying his best to fit into this world. It may have been his renegade behavior that attract me to him. Perhaps, I was wanting to play the role of a savior, or it was my unconscious need to be needed. Little did I know that the one needing to be saved was myself.

He appeared to be immersed in a battle with his own personal demons, which required most of his energy. This was often expressed as disharmony at home. The love I so desired from others was not coming from him, either. His need for acceptance was my own need; he was my mirror.

Of course, rather than being guided into discovery of self-love and standing in my own power, the ego part of my mind dug into my subconscious and came up with an old, familiar solution. Maybe if I was sick, my husband would pay more attention to me and show me that he cared. This would reinforce the guilt in me and in him. Yep, that will do it! Manifesting disease in my body, specifically created as symbol of guilt is piled on with more guilt, making the energetic flow stagnate and blocked. An ideal recipe for sickness.

The need to feel loved, accepted, and wanted caused me to fall back on my childhood lesson. This was a cycle that seemed to repeat itself over and over. This ego solution now had the potential of being a very real threat to the body, adding more chains to imprisoning and confining the mind in this world. How could happiness possibly come out of this pattern? I spent many years going from doctor to doctor having many misdiagnoses. A common diagnosis was depression. I was sent to a psychiatrist because, apparently, it was all in my mind. Little did I know then, there was much truth to that diagnosis, except I couldn't understand how there could be so much pain in the body. It was a sick mind, indeed!

Finally, thirty years later, after seeking help from all kinds of doctors, having several surgeries, losing a lot of weight, looking like I was on death's door, there was a diagnosis of Celiac disease. The body's ability to absorb essential nutrients was no longer functioning. There's a list of consequential diseases that could follow if this problem is not addressed before all the organs start to shut down. My mind had decided to start withholding the flow of life, shutting down the availability of energetic nourishment for the body, by consistently creating more solid energy blockages.

The negative thinking within the mind caused many issues with reproductive organs, activating a blockage of the flow of creativity. Lack of self-love and any other love would definitely choke any desire of life. I was increasingly having problems with my memory, unable to think clearly about simple daily functions. Becoming extremely frightened and completely distraught, when I couldn't remember my children's names. My sick mind activated the shutting down of the body by slowly removing its awareness.

During Time Line Therapy classes, we did an exercise with a partner, attempting to heal a health problem. I was told to visualize, holding in my right hand, a symbolic representation of a health issue I wished to address. The health issue was the arthritis in my fingers, and the chosen symbolism was *a chunk of iron*. When asked, why I thought *a chunk of iron* best represented the arthritis; my response was, "It did not bend, it was unbreakable."

I realized my decision to be inflexible was caused by a determination to prevent my *will* from being broken, ultimately manifesting as energy blockages in my body. During the many distressful times, there were countless moments when my will to live was barely hanging on. My survival depended on being ridged and firm, holding my ground. My body was mirroring what was going on in my mind.

Unfortunately, the belief that caused the decisions to be inflexible was not fully healed. There are many situations, not only in this life, but also in previous lives, which require addressing before all foolish thoughts and behaviors are completely released. These would include the accumulation of frequently feeling unworthy, unloved and being a victim, which is completely opposite to the reality of my True Self. Sickness never brought me the love or specialness I searched for most of my life.

I had to go through a self-made hell before I could learn that what I was looking for outside of myself was within me. It was important to love myself and learn that I was as special as everyone else. No one is more special; all are fragments of the same mind. We are all the same, desperately needing healing and guided direction for a way out of this painful world.

There may be many lifetimes of very destructive self-abusive thinking and behaviors that would require accessing the unconscious mind, to be identified, resolved, and healed. It is essential to be vigilant with all thoughts and behaviors, in order that the mind isn't endlessly crucified by projecting guilt onto another body, adding more layers to the existing unconscious wrong mindedness.

What is seemingly lacking in ourselves is searched out in our partners. A common lack is self-love. We look for others who will not only love us, but who will affirm their love through their actions and behaviors. When my husband no longer fulfilled his unconscious contract to shower me with love, I responded with feelings of rejection and abandonment, causing sadness, depression, and guilt. Guilt for many things, but the bottom line is that this is the same guilt that started the whole mess; the wrong thinking imbedded in the mind in the first place with the initial thought of separation.

*"Sickness is not an accident. Like all defenses, it is an insane device for self-deception. And like all the rest, its purpose is to hide reality, attack it, change it, render it inept, distort it, twist it, or reduce it to a little pile of unassembled parts. The aim of all defenses is keeping the truth from being whole. The parts are seen as if each one were whole with itself."*[1]

154

Sickness is the ego's strongest psychological tool. The mind *believes* that it is a body and is constantly fearing death. Sickness consumes the mind, leaving no room for considering other possibilities of Truth. The mind is completely distracted and not remotely interested in questioning the reality of it all.

Sickness fulfills a specific purpose in the mind. The mind imagines the body being sick; then, creates that reality. The body is submitted to all kinds of treatments and surgeries, unconsciously drawing others into the journey toward healing. Nevertheless, it is the search for love, attention from others that the mind is really desiring and needing, in an attempt to fill a void. What is dearly lacking is self-love. There isn't an awareness of this agenda since it is all unconscious. It's the *journey toward healing* that carries a sadistic need, which feeds a sickness that is clearly only in the mind.

The inability to love oneself, drives the mind to seek for love and attention outside itself. Sickness causes others to rally around them, giving emotional support through their loving concerns and prayers. The real problem, which is in the mind, is constantly sustained and fed by the continuation of seeking the attention and special treatment that sickness provides.

*Munchausen Syndrome by Proxy* is an extreme example of this mental problem. An article in the *Michigan Medicine - University of Michigan*, presents helpful information regarding this form of mental illness.[2] Caregivers, usually a parent, fabricate or cause health problems in vulnerable people, for which they are responsible. They intentionally create health crisis' in others; then, go through the process of appearing to seek help for their loved ones (victims), while aggrandizing themselves in the illusion of power and control. Solely to gain sympathy, love and attention, as well as fulfilling a need to feel important and significant. All of these virtues are dearly lacking in their sick minds.

The drawing of the mind's constant thoughts to sickness and concerns by others, keeps *everyone* entrapped within this illusionary dream. Sickness serves the ego's purpose by nourishing and sustaining the existence of this world. Lack of self-love, a pandemic in this world, is the cause of many problems, both individually and globally.

# HOW DOES THE BODY SERVE THE AWAKENING?

Science of medicine is used to treat illness in a body. All types of healing are inclusive and play their part in miracle interventions, attempting to heal a variety of sicknesses. There are numerous treatments, many tests, scans, surgeries, and drugs. Along with many other accepted medical interventions included in this group is healing through acupuncture, reflexology, massage therapy, physiotherapy, naturopathic therapy, and spiritual healing of which there is a variety of techniques available. The mind's belief that it is helpful, plays a big role in the healing process.

All medical assistance are forms of energy manipulations within the body. These are all miracle treatments that have the potential to infiltrate, alter, break-up, transform, and possibly eliminate the energy blockages. All interventions along with an intense belief within the mind that they will succeed, could, indeed, heal and cure sickness within a body. Surgeries and transplants are a testament to many diseases appearing to be cured.

We are all aware of experiments with sugar pills, a placebo, given to patients. If one believes they will help, they may very well help. The mind is convinced that it will be effective. If the underlying true cause of sickness, which is *only* in the mind, does not change; then, the illness or energy blocks could show up in a different location, or morph into a different form to eventually kill the body.

The body is a means through which one can escape this dream and awaken to truth. It becomes a learning tool for the mind along with assistance, which is always available upon request, from the Holy Spirit/ Higher Self and/or Spirit Guides. Help may come as a thought, if one could get in the space between the ego's constant run of thoughts, while meditating, in a dream, or as synchronistic events. One is never alone on this journey.

When the mind's thoughts are of love, prayer, or communication with Jesus, the energy of the body vibrates at a higher frequency. Conversely, when the mind has a thought of hate, regret, guilt, blame, jealousy, self-hatred, judgement, or criticism the vibration of the body slows down, causing energy blocks resulting as manifestations of sickness in the body.

Becoming aware of the consequent sicknesses within the body caused by specific negative mindedness, gives the mind an opportunity to alter its thinking and behaviors; thus, presenting opportunities to heal the mind and body. It is essential for the mind to transform its thinking, realigning with its True Self before anything changes.

*"It's a choice you make, a plan you lay, when for an instant truth arises in your own deluded mind, and all your world appears to tatter and prepare to fall. Now are you sick, that truth may go away and threaten your establishments no more."*[3]

When the occasion does arise and we start to question *what is* and want something *different*, the ego may very well choose illness to distract us. I have experienced the ego doing just that. Within a few weeks, I experienced headaches, sinus issues, skin rashes, precancerous skin lesions, bladder infections, along with sickness and health problems affecting loved ones.

A whole lot of drama and stress continued, as my attention shifted to my sister's sickness, ambulance trips, hospitals, tests, and doctor's appointments. All hell broke loose! The ego was fighting for its life. I have been determined not to allow ego to draw me back into this illusion; however, I suspect it could be a battle to the end.

Sickness consumes our thoughts and brings on the accompanying obsessive thinking that the ego desires. We are distracted by the ego's script and its life is secured when sickness is the focus. This buys the ego time to reaffirm and re-establish itself back into the mind's belief system. It may take some time before the mind once again questions life as it is and looks for other possible truths.

Sickness makes the body real to the mind and awareness of pain dominates all thoughts. Your loved ones and medical staff rally around you, sustaining the illusion in their lives as well. All magic surgeries, pills and therapy will work, temporarily, as healing appears to occur. Correction in the mind is essential for healing to be permanent. No magic pill will undo the false belief of separation from the Source.

If your life doesn't seem to be working and you feel trapped in a pattern, it's time to say to yourself, "There must be a better way." Don't expect others to change. The change must take place within you first; then, you will see it in others. Start changing the way you look at things and the things you look at will also change. Otherwise, the cycle of life and death will continue until one can no longer bear it. This is when an intense desire to go Home is much stronger than the chains that bind you to this illusionary world.

*"The body is the means by which God's Son returns to sanity. Though it was made to fence him into hell without escape, yet has the goal of Heaven been exchanged for the pursuit of hell. The Son of God extends his hand to reach his brother, and to help him walk along the road with him. Now is the body holy. Now it serves to heal the mind that it was made to kill."*[4]

The body's interactions with other bodies gives the mind an opportunity for release from imprisonment within the dream. It is essential to recognize the projection and mirroring process, to practice true forgiveness and embrace the love of your brother, who is really you, separated and equally broken.

The body is used as a vehicle for salvation with the acceptance of Atonement, or act of love innately within one's mind. This happens by releasing the inner Light, projecting it onto others and accepting the Truth that others are merely a reflection of oneself.

CHAPTER

# 21

# HOW DO THOUGHTS, BELIEFS, AND BEHAVIORS CONTRIBUTE TO DISEASE IN A BODY?

*"It is your thoughts alone that cause you pain. Nothing external to your mind can hurt or injure you in anyway. There is no cause beyond yourself that can reach down and bring oppression. No one but yourself affects you. There is nothing in the world that has the power to make you ill or sad, or weak or frail. But it is you who have the power to dominate all things you see by merely recognizing what you are."*

ACIM[1]

There is nothing outside of your mind that can hurt you, or cause you pain. The cause is excessive thoughts, holding onto past hurts, and unwillingness to forgive. It is your thoughts of judgment, criticism, self-punishment, and all other negative beliefs. There is a tendency to have our guard up, ready to defend the exposure of our inner guilt. We are all broken, all of us make mistakes; it's part of the learning process.

Emotions, thoughts, and life in this universe are all made of energy, continuously recycled in a transformed state. Nothing remains stagnate. With every breath, atoms that compose our inner organs are exchanged with atoms from other bodies. There is a constant exchange of information with everything in this universe. Health of the mind and body depends on a free and balanced universal movement of giving and taking.

Several resources, medical journals and informational sites mention that changes are repeatedly taking place within the human body every day. An article by *Angela Epstein* in the *Daily Mail - Health*, discusses the many changes in the body, the constant cell changes and rejuvenations of various organs.[2] The cells of the lungs are renewed every 2-3 weeks and need about a year to be completely renewed. The liver is renewed every 150 days and it is suggested that if 70% of the liver is removed, within 2 months 90% grows back. Our organs, blood, skin, and skeletal makeup are constantly changing; atoms continually regenerating and producing new cells. Physicists and Scientists suggest that as much as 98% of the body's atoms are replaced within a year. Our DNA is regularly changing and the body you had 6 -7 years ago is not the same today, nor will it be 7 years from now. When 98% of our bodies are replaced each year, why are we not cured of our health issues?

There could be a combination of past life's unresolved issues, personal or ancestral karma, and generational beliefs and behaviors manifesting as genetic diseases in a body. Memories of emotional wounds, which caused the karma are filed away in the unconscious mind, rearing their ugly heads, now and then, hoping to be acknowledged, released, and healed. The beliefs brought into this life experience, along with negative behaviors added onto previous ones, play a big role in determining the health of a body.

Drugs and medical treatments are only temporary. Even when the body appears to have been healed and freed of disease if wrong mindedness is not corrected, a disease will reappear in the body. Since no adjustments are made within thoughts and beliefs, the energy blocks will continue to be renewed, rebuilt, and build upon themselves, ultimately leading to the body's demise.

All diseases are sickness in the mind projected into a body, a manifestation of guilt into form. All causation is in the mind. If the disease is not cured but the mind has been actively working on changing beliefs and behaviors, it will have progressed on its path to awakening. It's awareness will leave the body and this universe with a changed personality, no longer needing to repeat specific lessons. Thus, the mind will be closer to a state of being healed; therefore, lessening the number of essential life experiences.

# GENETIC DISEASES

There is no such thing as blood relations. Those who act the parts of our family members are just parts of the same separated mind, projected out into bodies and this universe for the same purpose of learning and healing. There is merely an appearance of a relationship represented by extension and projection of bodies. It is simply, the mind's awareness of a continuation of a life's journey through a body; a part of a fractured mind working together with other parts of the same fractured mind. The Spirit within the fractured mind is equally fragmented and serves as a guide in assisting with healing and reconnecting all fragmented parts.

Right from the beginning, intimate relationships with parents and siblings set the stage for life's learning. The seemingly inheritances are played out through the mind's memory of previous beliefs, life experiences, ancestral and personal karma. Even though beliefs and behaviors of those closest to the personality add to one's character, personal emotional baggage from past life experiences contribute greatly. How the separated mind reacted in the past, in regard to treatment of oneself and others is a contributing factor, which is also brought into this lifetime.

The saying *the sins of the father are revisited by the son,* means that every generation has an opportunity to change *what always was.* Once again, I need to be clear, there are no such things as *sins.* There is no need for repentance, nor does anyone need to be crucified. Had the father seen the error of his ways, the son would not have to go down the same path of learning. Not only would one be healing oneself, but future generations may also be spared that life lesson.

Within an interplay of a family of bodies, memories can be generational memories, brought from past experiences. The scientific and medical community tells us it is passed down through our DNA. Nevertheless, the body is nothing, a mere thought and a *symbol* of guilt. It is the fractured mind's remembrance and continuation of repetitive negative thinking and beliefs that are projected out into (future fractured minds) *their children's* minds. If these thought systems remain unaltered, energy blocks will continue to be created in bodies and manifest as genetic diseases in future generations. All layers of wrong mindedness would have to be stripped down and healed.

Negativity is brought about by one's warped perceptions. Generations of conditioning and programmed beliefs are layered by more beliefs until the filters through which one views the world is completely distorted and flawed. It is the result of one fractured mind, fracturing itself repeatedly, projecting the same guilt rather than owning and healing it. One of the places to start is to change the way one thinks. It is necessary to arm oneself with wisdom, to be open to new perspectives, possibilities, and be prepared to break away from all preconceived beliefs.

Not only individuals, but also family groups are able to progress or regress. It all depends on choices that are made. If a parent's wrong mindedness leads to alcoholism and consequent health issues, and if one of his or her children chooses to think and behave differently, addictive tendencies will no longer potentially be passed onto their future generations. If another child adopts the same negative thinking as the parent, odds are good that his or her road will also lead towards addictive tendencies and potentially be passed on to their line of future generations.

Genetic diseases could skip a generation or not, depending on whether the individuals, parts of the group, progress or regress. It is also possible to do one; then, the other during another life experience. Two steps forward and one step back is one of many choices that are made while dancing through life. It all depends on whether there is a determination to progress and change negative beliefs, or to keep doing the same old, same old. Because of the veil of forgetfulness with which we come into this world, it is extremely difficult to choose to learn new ways. Change is extremely challenging and intimidating for the mind. New ways appear to be complicated, take focus, determination, and a deep desire to learn new sequences of steps essential for a different way of dancing through life.

# OUR BODIES COME WITH A BUILT-IN GPS SYSTEM

The mind's awakening is a progressive movement through healing, which comes in stages of detachment from a belief in a body and world.

The body was created to serve as a scapegoat, a projection of the initial guilt imagined within the mind, a crazy idea of wanting to be special. The mind firmly believes that the body is responsible for all consequential emotional repercussions. It is convinced that this emotional pain is caused by the body's thinking and behavior and believes it is the effect and the body is the cause; thus, refusing to take responsibility for any problems. This is not possible, of course, since the body and world are creations in the mind. The truth is that the mind is the cause and the body is the effect. The accepted repeated behavior of projecting guilt out onto others, continues to sustain the existence of the world.

The ego mind is the self-proclaimed king of an illusionary world. It is a powerful ruler, firmly controlling, and demanding that its thought system is completely integrated into everyday life. It will not hesitate to engage in ruthless battles to the end, if necessary, to maintain its kingdom. There may be a loss of some bodies in the process; however, this would only serve to inject more fear and more control over other bodies.

The ego works diligently in sustaining fear, pain, guilt, hate, and an attack environment during its seemingly endless reign. It creates a necessity for a mind to be always vigilant, incessantly suspicious of others, all who could be dangerous and should be feared. From a personal perspective, one's own mind is always the innocent one, all others are guilty.

There are many avenues, or spirit-lines though which assistance is available, for healing the mind. These are purposefully placed within a body, to be accessed when the mind desires to awaken from this dream. One of the spirit-lines available for this awakening process could be symbolized by a GPS system, which is put in place upon the birth of a new life cycle. Imagine discs containing crucial memories, truths that were obscured by a veil of forgetfulness upon re-entering a body to experience a life. Precious gifts of memory that have been filed away and nearly forgotten.

A programmed guidance system containing important necessary information in order to trigger a memory in the mind. Much like a popular game called Geo-caching, GPS coordinates lead to discs, which contain gifts of insights, referenced as a memory cache. Memory cache, in the age of computers, is computer storage that is used to quickly retrieve frequently used information. Geo describes the global nature of activity.

These caches, which are full of *Light* energy were projected into a body and strategically placed, so they are easily assessable in order to activate dramatic changes within the mind's thinking. These are spiritual insights necessary for healing and nullifying potential energy blocks caused by patterns of misconceptions and wrong belief systems. The guidance system tracks through a maze of possible misdirected pathways, detours, and stops, as the GPS system of the mind's vehicle (the body) is continually recalculating and redirecting back onto a more direct route Home.

The journey to reconnect with its True Self; then, is mapped through co-ordinances, as a guidance system along the back bone, the spine of a body. Similar to a system we may be familiar with, called the Chakra System. The memory discs; however, utilizes the body in assisting with an awakening of a memory in the mind; a specific Truth that the *body* and *universe* are *not real*. Each memory cache is a containment of essential explicit spiritual intelligence and wisdom. A remembrance available to be embraced at any time during one's life, slowly dissolving the veil of forgetfulness to reveal a forgotten Truth.

There are certain times in one's life that serve as opportunities for choices and changes. Negative behaviors directing one down a precarious path manifest as energy blockages in a specific part of a body. Diseases in that location, would be an indication to correct particular beliefs and behaviors that are not in line with wisdom within that particular co-ordinating Spiritual Cache.

Wrong-mindedness creates an opportunity for pockets of negative energy to become concentrated. If negative thinking exist, they will continue to strengthen the veil of forgetfulness, keeping the truth concealed and inaccessible. The flow of positive *Light* energy becomes unavailable; therefore, unable to sustain the life of the body. This is when the energy blocks would cause sicknesses eventually leading to death.

Sickness is a wake-up call. If one needs help to reprogram the direction taken, the memory wisdom discs give guidance and present opportunities to choose again. This re-routing is important in changing direction of one's path, allowing a free flow of positive energy through a diseased area in a body. When the mind is in sync with the Truth of its Reality, which would be a Truth contained in each Spiritual Disc, the energy flow is constant and uninterrupted.

This guidance could be likened to loving touches, gently redirecting, and enticing an onward movement to a full awakening. This system is greatly needed as the world moves toward a global awakening during the Aquarian Age.

# EGO'S AGENDA

The ego has its own agenda. Its very existence depends on compromising the programmed route, by jamming and inundating it with alternative routes and unplanned side trips. Many of them are added to coincide with the ego's immediate needs; ego is always searching for instant gratification.

It may suggest visiting the mall because it senses the always nagging feeling of lack. Does making a purchase one doesn't need or ill afford, fill that void? It may bring some happiness, but only until you get the bill! Having to address lack of funds would cause discord, stress, anxiety, and perhaps an unhappy trip to the bank quickly followed by marriage counselling.

Conflict at home results in a visit to the school principal to address psychological problems in your children. This very quickly snowballs into a trip to court, for divorce proceedings and resolutions of financial child support and custody issues. Dealing with all this strife may now require anti-depressants and counselling. Adding to all the other drama, one of your family members is perhaps dealing with addiction issues, your teenager is involved with drugs, or you are coping with a death of a loved one.

Where were you going? What was the original destination? At this time there could be a *wake-up* call, an accident or sickness within the body. In truth, it is your Spirit realizing that the direction you were going was getting you nowhere, fast. In complete desperation, you call out to an unseen entity, "Help Me!" Only then, you may be compelled to clear and delete all the ego's distracting and negative routes from the body's GPS.

This would be a long process. A lot of correction is required in the mind before recollecting its intended destination and how to retrieve the programmed direct route. It requires a firm intention, determination, tremendous fortitude, and a desire to stay on that route. Intense focus, spiritual guidance, and inner work is essential in order to be in a place of receptivity of necessary wisdom within each memory disc. Quieting one's thoughts and having deep conversations with a Spirit Guide, Higher Self, Holy Spirit, or Jesus would be helpful. This may take several hundreds of life experiences, solely because of the ego's determination to keep itself alive; thus, it will continue to redirect.

When the *wake-up* call comes, as sickness in an organ, awareness of its location within the mind's vehicle, the body, makes it easier to address possible mental causes. You could revisit those thoughts, beliefs, and behaviors related to that area and choose to change that *wrong-mindedness* behavior and heal the resulting chaos manifesting in the body.

With the help of your Spirit Guides or Jesus, it is possible to get back on track to retrieve forgotten memory, access the original coordinates, and reprogram the GPS to your intended destination. Once the beliefs and behaviors are fully integrated into the mind and are in sync with memory of the True Self and True Reality; then, the mind will awaken onto Self.

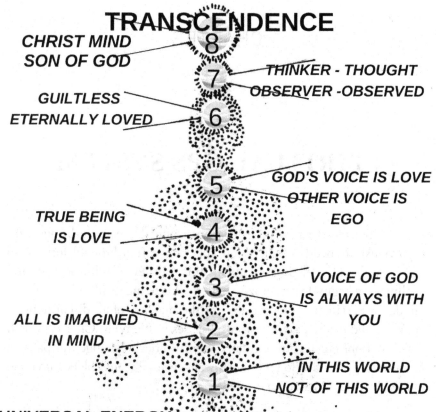

TRANSCENDENCE

CHRIST MIND
SON OF GOD

8

7

THINKER - THOUGHT
OBSERVER - OBSERVED

GUILTLESS
ETERNALLY LOVED

6

5

GOD'S VOICE IS LOVE
OTHER VOICE IS
EGO

TRUE BEING
IS LOVE

4

3

VOICE OF GOD
IS ALWAYS WITH
YOU

ALL IS IMAGINED
IN MIND

2

1

IN THIS WORLD
NOT OF THIS WORLD

UNIVERSAL ENERGY
CONSTANTLY
MOVING THROUGH
AND
INTERCHANGING
WITH ENERGY
OF THE BODY

SPIRITUAL
MEMORY
CACHE

# CHAPTER

# 22

# SPIRITUAL GPS SYSTEM

The personality returning to a birth and death cycle brings with it previously imbedded beliefs and ancestral karma brought forward to be resolved and healed. Throughout this journey of self-discovery and healing, one begins to recognize a pattern. There are similarities in wrong mindedness, which are responsible for the majority of all disharmony in one's life and core causes of various diseases in the body. Choices, which life's situations create, give multiple opportunities to change this pattern. Negative energy draws to itself more negative energy; they blend and meld into each other. Change is required.

## FIRST SPIRITUAL DISC

# MEMORY CACHE:

## Remembrance:

*One is in this world - Not of this world.*

# Spiritual Wisdom:

*The Mind is outside Time and Space and encompasses all things within Time and Space.*

*The body and universe exist only within the Mind.*

# Meditation:

*"I am as God created me. I am God's Son. Today I lay aside all sick illusions of myself, and let my Father tell me Who I really am."*[1]

## Prayer:

*"It is impossible to see two worlds. Let me accept the strength God offers me and see no value in this world, that I may find my freedom and deliverance.*

*How can illusions satisfy God's Son? Father, the truth belongs to me. My home is set in Heaven by Your Will and mine. Can dreams content me? Can illusions bring me happiness? What but Your memory can satisfy Your Son? I will accept no less than You have given me. I am surrounded by Your Love, forever still, forever gentle and forever safe. God's Son must be as You created him.*

*Today we pass illusions by. And if we hear temptation call to us to stay and linger in a dream, we turn aside and ask ourselves if we, the Sons of God, could be content with dreams, when Heaven can be chosen just as easily as hell, and love will happily replace all fear."* [2]

Energy blocks caused by *wrong mindedness* manifest as sickness within the area of the body where the *First Disc* is located. Parts of the body possibly affected:

The base of the spine, the rectum, hips, bones, feet and legs, varicose veins and the immune system. Cancer and various problems located in those areas of the body.

The **First Memory Cache of *Light*** is situated at the base of the body's frame, along its supportive backbone, the spine. This is an important opportunity for ego to firmly cement a strong presence within a body. The ego needs a solid hold on mind's beliefs in order to secure its imprisonment within the illusion. The body serves as a fence, keeping love and potential attackers out, enforcing separation.

Since the body was created as a symbol of guilt and fear, it is designed to have the belief ingrained that fear is always biting at one's heels. There is a constant need to be ready for confrontation, to run, kill, or do whatever it takes to ensure the survival of the body. Danger, fear, sickness, and death are constant companions of one's life. There's a frequent *flight or fight* state, intending to keep the mind entrenched in the illusionary world, entangled with one immediate and urgent situation after another.

The ego nurtures importance of belonging to a separate family of bodies, connecting with the universe, grounding with Mother-Earth, and instilling attachments to materialistic comforts of the world. There is deep association with specific group mentality, especially the immediate family and all other influential energies that are more prominently at play during the early developmental stages of one's life. Previous beliefs and attachments to the world are an important integral part of the building blocks of the foundation of this life's experience.

Acceptance of the immediate family's disparaging beliefs would cause the spiritual groundwork to be very shaky and may dictate a life of rebuilding a more solid and stable foundation. All previously gained forward movements of one's spiritual awareness is also brought into this life experience. Throughout lifetimes there is a continuation of building upon past progress, and moving closer to discovering one's True Reality.

The mind's belief that it is a body and that the universe is real, makes it a challenge to comprehend which beliefs are worth following and keeping. Preconditioned and accepted beliefs could take one on a journey in the opposite direction, rather than a path towards discovering one's inner *light*.

Right from the beginning of life, the ego is the driving force in everyday decision making. The personality, the mask one wears and presents to the world, is ego created and sustained.

Do inherited family values include a stable spiritual foundation with responsibility for a global family? Perhaps you simply accept your family's religious beliefs, never questioning the authenticity. Do you believe it is possible to *sin*? Do you believe God would sacrifice one of His sons for the lives of His other sons? Would you?

Jesus' words on the cross were, *"Father, forgive them, for they do not know what they do."* It's interesting that in the 21st century, humanity's (mind's) beliefs and behaviors still reflect ignorance. It's a choice to not know. It is time to question the drivers of our decision-making-process and discover the answers to *why we do what we do,* take personal responsibility and change. It may be time to question the blind faith of old established beliefs and consider entertaining other possibilities, bravely stepping outside the circle of comfort and dare to think differently.

It is not easy to break free from a pattern of established family values and expectations. The need for acceptance and approval makes it challenging to break free from preconditioned thinking. Not wanting to disappoint our loved ones along with fear of rejection causes us to conform. We find it problematic to stand in our own power and bravely attempt to achieve the reality of our passions and dreams.

Family discord can threaten one's security and cause fear of being alone. Obsessive, compulsive behavioral patterns may be driven by anxiety, fear, and feeling insecure in one's environment. Fear imprisons one in continual darkness. It is important to strive to step out of the darkness and choose to follow the light.

Being a victim of abusive behavior, whether psychological or physical, robs one of power. A lack of self-worth, self-respect makes it difficult to be assertive and independent. Depression, repression, and denial of self-value is exasperated by focusing on negative thoughts of self-hatred and self-punishment. A sense of paranoia and powerlessness leaves one in a constant state of vulnerability and completely oblivious of Self-Truth.

An incapability of taking responsibility for personal unhappiness triggers needless suffering. Believing outside circumstances are to blame for one's misfortunes only serves the ego mind. Not being able to learn from a situation, choosing instead to take the stance of victimhood, entraps one in an unbreakable cycle of blame, self-pity and anger. Nurturing such unproductive notions places one at the whim of life's circumstances, causing stagnation, a loss of personal control, self-respect, and self-value making it difficult to break the cycle of negativity.

What about groups outside the immediate family circle? Are their beliefs and behaviors questioned? The importance of being accepted and belonging to a group may lead one to be unduly pressured into questionable behaviors. Insecurities drive a need to conform to expectations, to fit in, creating a susceptibility to the influence of others. It takes a lot of courage to step outside an established circle of group mentality and stand firmly and bravely on one's own two feet.

The state of comfort in a body in this world greatly affects choices. By idolizing the human body, constantly augmenting it's appearance by following, obsessing, and layering it with ever-changing materialistic trends is an attempt to measure up to ego's perception of beauty. Our desire to conform to what is seen as *the ideal body image* drives the constantly changing health and clothing industry, which in turn works to further distract us from seeking knowledge of who we really are. This both influences and dictates blind faith within the mass psyche, drawing the mind further into the illusion. How much of an impact do these materialistic values have on you?

Is there an innate sense of being a stranger in this world, simply not belonging here? Established beliefs and influences create a form of normalcy in acceptance of dividedness and separateness. Complacency prevents one from realizing the detrimental harm societal influences exert toward a disinterest in seeking other truths, and the critical roles they play in paving *one's path* and *time frame* for an awakening unto Self. The ego will continue to place hurdles and distractions on your spiritual path in order to keep you entrenched in its world.

Ancestral karma keeps one locked in behaviors creating a constant struggle to release throughout many lifetimes. Discovering a history of genetic diseases and understanding possible accompanying beliefs and behaviors would assist greatly with recognizing the mental drivers of those behaviors. Actively implementing the changes within one's thinking and beliefs would prevent a repeat of those diseases.

How much importance is placed on your ancestral legacy? You do inherit royalty, but it is the kingdom of God, rather than in this illusionary universe. Perhaps it is an unconscious memory, innately within the mind, that drives a desire to reconnect with one's True Self. Are you skeptical of a belief in a Divine Plan or Spiritual Beings? Is it possible to entertain the likelihood that God is *not* the creator of this universe, and that the personal mind creates our world? Is proof required before you would consider other probabilities? What happened to blind faith?

## SECOND SPIRITUAL DISC

# MEMORY CACHE

## Remembrance:

*The Universe and Bodies are a Creative Thought.*
*A Thought imagined in a Delusional Mind.*

## Spiritual Wisdom:

*The Mind supplies the Creative Energy.*
*The Fractured Mind is the Cause, the Body and World are the Effect.*

## Meditation:

*"My Self is ruler of the universe. It is impossible that anything should come to me unbidden by myself. Even in this world, it is I who rule my destiny.*

*What happens is what I desire. What does not occur is what I do not want to happen. This must I accept. For thus am I led past this world to my creations, children of my will, in Heaven where my holy Self abides with them and Him Who has created me."* [3]

# Prayer:

*"The Son of God is my Identity. Father, You know my true Identity. Reveal It now to me who am Your Son, that I may waken to the truth in You, and know that Heaven is restored to me."* [4]

**Energy blocks caused by *wrong mindedness* manifest as sickness within the area of the body where the *Second Disc* is located. Parts of the body possibly affected:**

Many diseases involving the sexual organs, ovarian, reproduction, menstrual problems, endometriosis, vaginal infections, prostate difficulties, impotency and venereal diseases, cancers, sciatica, issues with lower back, slipped, ruptured and bulging discs, pelvic area.

The **Second Memory Cache of *Light*** is positioned just below the navel, above the First Disc, in the area of the reproductive organs. Energy blocks created by wrong mindedness affect organs within this space. The ego mind continues to focus on securing the existence of its world. It affirms a belief that others are to blame for our disharmony and does its best to keep projection active and prominent. It guarantees its survival by a body's ability to create more bodies in order to produce other egos. There is a determination to instill the importance of the mind's belief in separation. Duality, individuality, a personal expression of ego, I, me, you, others, and an establishment of boundaries is firmly set in place. An effective motto of the ego is *to separate, divide and conquer.*

This rule of the ego world is augmented by instilling importance of materialistic acquisitions, mine, yours, theirs, financial achievements, establishing a position of psychological influences, and enforcing the authority of boundaries. Mine, my stuff, my religion, my family, my country, all are separate and different from what is yours, but that doesn't mean I respect your borders; I may want whatever is yours as well. The mentality of needing to establish a winner or a loser causes many imbalances. Outside group influences are prevalent and the potential consequences within one's mind play a significant role.

It is an appropriate time to question your values. Your day to day life could be consumed with attaining material possessions, accumulation of financial wealth and all other entrapments of this world. It is easy to be seduced by physical appearances and the mind's senses, driving a need for augmentation with materialistic things. It is all very alluring, but it is also very fleeting; everything is subject to change and could very quickly be taken away.

It may be important to be idolized, admired, or even feared. A need to express one's individuality, or to combat fear of being invisible, instigates a drive to establish a presence, to be noticed, and to feel important. Perhaps taking on the role of a joker, bully, the weak, or sick one. Lack of self-love and self-esteem prevents an awareness of one's True Reality, within which there are no lacks.

Lack of self-respect and self-worth leaves one vulnerable to outside stresses, easily being coerced into questionable behavior and swayed by others. Self-confidence, independent thinking, and self-assuredness offers protection from succumbing to the effects of fanatic religious groups such as cults. Do you commit to blind loyalty, or are you able to make your choices freely and stand in your personal power?

Outside groups play a major role in influencing the mind. Perhaps you seek the company of those who are successful, famous, and wealthy to raise your own self-image and importance. You may choose to wear an assortment of masks, forms of deception, as a way of fulfilling personal and financial needs. A necessity to feel superior to others causes an inability to handle relationships with equals. Do you try to influence others? Do you deal in good faith and are you trustworthy?

The constant feelings of lack in one's life drives a necessity to fill that void with sensual and material things, relationships, or adventures. Believing that one lacks anything, sustains a continuous quest for more, *keeping up with the Joneses* causing tremendous stress. These behaviors breed discord within family dynamics, personal relationships, and workplace. Discovering the frivolity of such pursuits often comes with the realization of a life wasted.

Immersing yourself in work at an expense of human relationships, would not be beneficial for your spiritual growth. Accumulation of material possessions may temporarily compensate for feelings of powerlessness. Perhaps you do not hesitate to sacrifice personal relationships for the climb up the financial and corporate ladder. Financial attainment would require sacrificing personal values as well. Is your worth dependant on materialistic things and will self-worth be lost if financial status is lost? When self-serving choices are made, they only prolong the *me, mine, and I*, treadmill of life.

Agreements made with marriage or life partners, influence decisions regarding *birthing* to future generations. Does one honor commitments to others? A relationship of any kind plays an important role in self-development and self-actualization. Unfortunately many relationships enter into a partnership expecting a fulfilment of a lack within oneself. "You complete me!" Is love conditional? If expectations aren't met, is one comfortable in bending the rules, not honoring agreements? Is adultery and abandonment acceptable?

You create tremendous harm to yourself and others when you choose to abuse sex or money. Controlling and manipulating others by withholding or forcing sexual activity causes a domino effect requiring urgent correction. Providing financial support could serve a sinister purpose for controlling others, or you may become increasingly resentful of those who demand and expect *your* financial support.

Frequently defending you race, gender, or sexual preference takes a toll on your well being. You may feel trapped in a body of a particular gender, a relationship, or life situation. Are you unable to be true to yourself because you *fear* rejection? Perhaps the influence of other people's opinions affects your ability to live your life freely, stifling self-expression.

When one is conscious of personal and global responsibility, there is a natural extension of generosity of money and time outside of the immediate family circle. Is one in touch with the emotional needs of others? It is worthier to choose friends who accept everyone and treat all equally with kindness, those who do not hesitate to help, defend, and love regardless of race, color of skin or status. An innate empathy is instinctively expressed without hesitation when there is an acceptance of oneness and connectedness to everything in this world.

Are you aware that your mind is the creator of the world you experience and believe you see? The ego creates problems to distract from investigating a spiritual lack, preventing a deeper search for answers regarding the mysteries of this life. It's important to look for answers outside the box, the norm, questioning and breaking away from established family and societal beliefs. Your mind's choices throughout life, influence the direction of paths taken and determine if several detours will be necessary.

## THIRD SPIRITUAL DISC

# MEMORY CACHE

## Remembrance:

*The Voice for God - Holy Spirit - is Always with You.*

## Spiritual Wisdom:

*Sacred Communication is Continuous.*

## Meditation:

*"God's Voice speaks to me all through the day. There is not a moment in which God's Voice ceases to call on my forgiveness to save me. There is not a moment in which His Voice fails to direct my thoughts, guide my actions and lead my feet. I am walking steadily on toward truth. There is nowhere*

*else I can go, because God's Voice is the only Voice and the only Guide that has been give to His Son."*[5]

## Prayer:

*"I call upon God's Name and on my own. Repeat God's Name, and all the world responds by laying down illusions. Every dream the world holds dear has suddenly gone by, and where it seemed to stand you find a star; a miracle of grace. The sick arise, healed of their sickly thoughts. The blind can see; the deaf can hear. The sorrowful cast off their mourning, and the tears of pain are dried as happy laughter comes to bless the world."*[6]

**Energy blocks caused by *wrong mindedness* manifest as sickness within the area of the body where the *Third Disc* is located. Parts of the body affected are:**

Liver, pancreas, gallbladder, kidney, stomach, spleen, abdomen, upper intestine, Celiac and Crohn's disease, Colitis and irritable bowel, colon blockages, diverticulitis, middle spine, diabetes, indigestion, eating disorders, common seasonal flu and colds, autoimmune diseases, and cancers of organs.

The **Third Memory Cache of *Light*** is situated above the Second Disc, directly above the navel area. The ego's intention is to fully entrench the mind within a world of time and space. It projects great influence over the mind, as it utilizes time and space to accentuate trauma of past imagined emotional infractions. It hooks by injecting thoughts of past hurts and gives them continuous life in a tortuous monologue within a stream of thoughts. Not only keeping them alive and well in the now, but also projecting them into possible future scenarios.

Thoughts of desired retaliations, or imagined potential hurts in the future, along with relentless companions of pain and guilt, sink the mind deeper into this world. Forgiveness and letting go of past hurts are difficult when thoughts are activated as a choice of weapons. Constant worry, about the future for oneself or others, is like drawing to oneself a canopy of darkness that envelopes and consumes the mind.

Now is the time to recognize the effects of preconditioned patterns entrenched in one's mind. An opportunity to analyze the reason for the constant pre-occupations with the same thoughts and emotions. This is a time to question and change opinions and beliefs in the mind, which have been the stumbling blocks to moving beyond the *what always was* and deal with *what is*.

Feelings of inadequacies play havoc in the mind, as one continually feels threatened by successes of others, which only accentuates the sense of lack of self-worth. You may seek the company of those who are self-confident and successful, in order to stand in their Light and shine brighter. This would sustain feelings of inadequacy and unconsciously foster a *loser* mentality giving it continuous life. Resulting in falling victim to depression, drawing the mind deeper into the illusion.

An inability to make decisions, results in self-criticism and judgement. The ego is very good at imbedding the *loser* mentality, a lack of self-esteem and self-respect leaves one vulnerable to outside influences. Taking out your resentment and self-hatred on your loved ones, abusing them verbally, emotionally, or physically could lead to self-punishment. Self-hatred is continuously, unconsciously nurtured and sustained.

Blaming others for disempowerment creates resentment, hurt, and anger. Not taking responsibility for one's own behavior, constantly blaming others is a big wrong-mindedness issue. How long do you hang on to perceived hurts? When you are on a continuous roller-coaster ride of negative behavior, processing emotions may be difficult. Falsely believing they will just go away, just leaves a lot of accumulated unhealed inner pain, setting the stage for energy blockages. What negative emotions are not being processed, preventing them from being digested and released? Self-blame and continuous self-punishment makes it difficult to hear the faint intuitive voice offering a lifeline.

Lack of self-love drives a constant need to do for others, wanting their respect, kindness, and love in return. This could easily lead to feelings of rejection and anger when they fail to show their appreciation, or start to take your kindness for granted. Fear of stepping into your personal power may cause you to search for others to make your decisions and provide care for you. Allowing others to be in control because of your imbalanced emotional needs results with an inability to *digest* and release the negative beliefs that maintain and sustain lack of self-love.

Unconsciously not wanting to heal, spurs a journey of *searching* for healing, invariably feeding the sick mind. Along with securing ties to a body and the illusion, the problem of *not loving oneself* puts one in a position of seeking love and attention from others who are carried along on this ride. Lack of self-healing could be part of an unconscious repressed fear of becoming whole.

Sickness in the body gives the mind an opportunity to reflect, reorganize, release, and heal emotional issues constantly consuming one's thoughts. It is at this time that you may become aware of spiritual beings ready and available to assist you through your life's journey. How open and receptive are you to their presence and subtle communications? If belief in these spiritual helpers does not exist, what will it take before you consider such a possibility?

Ignoring your intuition, or dismissing it as foolishness, may prevent you from accessing wisdom, which would accentuate your power of discernment. Your gut is an important communication Disc, assisting you in making decisions and helping you become aware that you are not alone. It is important to place less value on ego guidance and more value on intuition, the second voice you hear in your mind. This is your Higher Self trying to communicate with you. Perhaps you have difficulty believing in divine assistance and synchronistic events, or you feel unworthy of receiving such guidance. Is there an unconscious fear of drawing back to oneself all the projected fractured pieces of the mind?

## FOURTH SPIRITUAL DISC

# MEMORY CACHE

## Remembrance:

*Our True Reality is Love.*

## Spiritual wisdom:

Forgive. All are Guiltless. No-thing Happened.

The Body and Universe are Illusions.

## Meditation:

*"Today I claim the gifts forgiveness gives. I will not wait another day to find the treasures that my Father offers me. Illusions are all vain, and dreams are gone even while they are woven out of thoughts that rest on false perceptions. Let me not accept such meager gifts again today. God's Voice is offering the peace of God to all who hear and choose to follow Him. This is my choice today. And so I go to find the treasures God has given me."*[7]

## Prayer:

*"Begin.................. by thinking of someone you do not like, who seems to irritate you, or to cause regret in you if you should meet him; one you actively despise or merely try to overlook. It does not matter what the form your anger takes. You probably have chosen him already. He will do.*

*Now close your eyes and see him in your mind, and look at him a while. Try to perceive some light in him somewhere; a little gleam which you had never noticed. Try to find some little spark of brightness shining through the ugly picture that you hold of him. Look at this picture until you see a light somewhere within it, and then try to let this light extend until it covers him, and makes the picture beautiful and good.*

*Look at this changed perception for a while, and turn your mind to one you call a friend. Try to transfer the light you learned to see around your former "enemy" to him. Perceive him now as more than friend to you, for in that light his holiness shows you your savior, saved and saving, healed and whole.*

*Then let him offer you the light you see in him, and let your "enemy" and friend unite in blessing you with what you gave. Now are you one with them, and they with you. Now have you been forgiven by yourself. Do not forget, throughout the day, the role forgiveness plays in bringing happiness to every unforgiving mind, with yours among them. .......... tell yourself:*

*Forgiveness is the key to happiness. I will awaken from the dream that I am mortal, fallible and full of sin, and know I am the perfect Son of God."*[8]

**Energy blocks caused by *wrong mindedness* manifest as sickness within the area of the body where the *Fourth Disc* is located. Parts of the body possibly affected are:**

The shoulders and arms, skeletal and muscular system, ribs, chest, diaphragm, bronchial and lung problems, pneumonia, asthma, and diseases of the breast, cancer, diseases of the heart, circulation problems, blocked arteries, mitral valve prolapsed, congestive heart failure, heart attacks.

The **Fourth Memory Cache of *Light*** area is where the ego set its eyes on victory. Its location is directly in line, above the Third Disc, to the right of the physical heart; its major influence is Love. It is here that ego's greatest threat lies. It's life in an illusionary world relies on this greatest battle. Love is one's True Realty and is a fearless weapon.

Ego attempts to convince the mind that *it* loves it so much, it gifted it with a body onto which to project all imaged fear and guilt. This gift is the driver of the universe. True love is constantly lacking and illusive, kept alive only by a faint memory within the mind. Many lifetimes are spent in search for love in all the wrong places. The ego insists that love and hate can coexist in its world and that it is okay to take another life, in the name of family honor, or love of country. Now is a significant time to work on discriminating between what is truly valuable and what is not.

Projections of hate, anger, and guilt give continuous life to the illusion though chaos and turmoil, causing personal and global battles. Holding onto past hurts without forgiveness, guarantees ego victory. Resentment, bitterness, and anger causes layering of stagnate energy pockets and creating bigger blocks until they no longer can be contained. Unprocessed and unreleased feelings of betrayal set the stage for manifesting disease in the body.

The physical heart is the center of love. All expressions of love flow from the Source. It is a Spirit-Light-Force that flows through the mind and its creations, the body and universe. Love is extended outward through energetic essence infiltrating other bodies, as the mind attunes to its natural spiritual rhythm. An ancient memory imbedded deep within, waiting for an opportunity to embrace all minds as they awaken to their True Reality.

An inability to admit mistakes, prevents an opportunity to learn from them. The ego's mind would not want to be embarrassed by projecting an appearance of weakness in asking for help. It takes more strength to admit one needs help than to stay in denial and continue to live a lie. It becomes difficult to move beyond that stagnate state. Old habits and conditionings are hard to break.

Are you attuned to your inner desires? Are you aware of moments that bring you great joy, those that make your heart soar and time fly? Perhaps you have sacrificed *your* dreams for those of someone else. Feeling stuck in a situation and allowing circumstances to prevent you from following your choice in a life style or occupation, would result in a festering resentment. Being jealous of other people's accomplishments, their successes, loving relationships and happiness, creates depression, a big stumbling block for self-motivation and self-actualization.

Believing that others are guilty of something sinister and can't be trusted is augmented by the belief that all things in this universe are separate from you. This contributes to a behavior of persistently judging, criticizing and being prejudice toward *others*. Being suspicious and hateful toward those who are perceived as different causes damage to the heart, which is a symbol of love. Problems develop when one gets caught up in an accepted view of the masses. An inability to form one's own beliefs leaves one vulnerable to potential injury caused by these views, beliefs, and behaviors.

Personal desires get in the way of compassion and empathy. Selfishness prevents a willingness to help others. This is a spiritual injury against oneself. All are One. If courage or strength cannot be found to step out of that path, the evolution of the Soul will become stagnant; consequent healing of the mind will require many more lifetimes to complete.

Are you able to take responsibility for your part in the disintegration of a relationship? Unconsciously sabotaging relationships sustains a belief that you are unlovable or unworthy of love. Perhaps, you betrayed someone by not honoring your vows, or you were betrayed. Denying personal responsibility in life's predicament creates a constant flow of difficult relationships. When you choose to blame others and hold onto resentments, it becomes difficult to forgive. True forgiveness releases chains that bind you to those with whom you have an issue.

Understanding that the same attributes one is emotionally attracted to, or repulsed by in another person are actually contained, hidden, repressed, and denied within oneself. Have you grasped the concept of seeing your inner image mirrored in others? Issues that we refuse to address within ourselves are constantly projected onto others, and mirrored back to us, to be owned and healed. Look around you; it is your face you see.

*If one is lonely when alone, one is in bad company.* Why is it so difficult to love oneself? Feeling unworthy of love, happiness, and lack of self-love is the driver behind a persistent need for outside approval. Maybe you are fearful of being alone, choosing to be in a loveless relationship, or decide to withdraw into a life of loneliness to avoid risking rejection and heartbreak. You may avoid the pain, but you will surely miss the dance of life and progression of your Soul.

Have you healed your *inner child*? Are those hurts, beliefs, and behaviors being unconsciously passed down to your children and future generations? Even though true understanding of forgiveness may still be illusive, the intention behind the act is very important. It's time to embrace the fact that *others* are parts of *you*. Forgiveness of others is an act of forgiveness of oneself.

How healthy is your heart? Do you still have difficulty integrating true forgiveness into your daily life? If you fluctuate between love and hate and believe both can exist at the same time, this can contribute to an irregular pumping of the heart and consequential problems. Have you begun to emotionally detach from the daily dramas, taken off your blinders and opened your mind to other understandings and spiritual truths?

Hatred, anger, hurt, and an inability to forgive causes slow dense energy, like thickened molasses, desperately trying to flow through your arteries and veins; progressively getting thicker, hardening, and blocking the body's pathways to the heart. How much emotional baggage are you carrying? How suffocating is the weight of *unforgiveness* on your chest? Is it creating blockages of the flow of life force, harming the heart?

It may be time to implement into daily life the statement *do unto others as you do would like others to do unto you*. Even if you feel you have a right to be angry at someone, love them anyway. The easiest way to kill your enemy is to love them to death. It is extremely difficult to reject love, since that is what everyone seems to be lacking. You will eventually discover that it is *yourself* that needed forgiveness and love. *You* are disguised in another body.

Losing hope, loneliness, and intense grief can lead (literally) to a broken heart (heart attack). Frightened by a belief that the end of a body is the end of oneself, contributes greatly to grieving not only for loved ones but also for yourself. Not believing you will see your deceased loved ones again causes unbearable anguish. Actively seeking knowledge of truth brings an understanding that we follow a blueprint, a unique design, leading to an awakening of wisdom revealing the Truth of our Reality.

# MEMORY CACHE

## Remembrance:

*The Voice of God is always of Love. All other voices are those of the Ego.*

## Spiritual Wisdom:

*Holy Spirit is the communication-line between the Mind and God.*

*Choose the Voice of the Holy Spirit, the Second Voice you Hear.*

## Meditation:

*"Let me be still and listen to the truth.*

*Let my own feeble voice be still, and let me hear the mighty Voice for Truth Itself assure me I am God's perfect Son."* [9]

## Prayer:

*"Steady our feet, our Father. Let our doubts be quiet and our holy minds be still, and speak to us. We have no words to give to You. We would but listen to Your Word, and make it ours. Lead our practicing as does a father lead a little child along a way he does not understand. Yet does he follow, sure that he is safe because his father leads the way for him.*

*So do we bring our practicing to You. And if we stumble, You will raise us up. If we forget the way, we count upon Your sure remembering. We wander off, but You will not forget to call us back. Quicken our footsteps now, that we may walk more certainly and quickly unto You. And we accept the Word You offer us to unify our practicing, as we review the thoughts that You have given us."* [10]

**Energy blocks caused by *wrong mindedness* manifest as sickness within the area of the body where the *Fifth Disc* is located. Parts of the body possibly affected:**

Throat issues, headaches - issues with the neck vertebrae, esophagus, trachea, mouth, teeth, teeth clenching, TMJ, jaw problems - causing problems with chewing, mouth ulcers and gum problems, tonsils, swollen glands, thyroid problems, laryngitis, joint problems, spinal stenosis, scoliosis, bulging and/or herniated disc, cancer involving any of those areas.

The ego's grip on the mind is now loosened somewhat, but it does not give up. The **Fifth Memory Cache of *Light*** is located in the throat area, in line and above all previous discs. The ego is the first voice that speaks, its constant chatter tries to drown out the Higher Self, making it impossible to get a word in edgewise. This voice serves to confuse, distract, and lure the mind deeper into illusion with a carrot masked with promises of happiness attached to materialistic things of this world.

It is a voice of deceit, as it layers disguises and covers up the cruelty of bodies and this world. It constantly injects fear, anger, and self-guilt into the mind, in a relentless mirage of past, present, and possible future imagined conversations and events. It is the voice used to inflict blame, pain, fear, and hatred onto other bodies, and turns love into hate with a slew of ugly, hurtful, and destructive words. The ego created other languages in furthering its agenda of enforcing separation. Words lose a lot of their true meaning in translation, causing confusion and misinterpretation, making it difficult for true communication, furthering the separation of bodies and countries.

Physical hands are *voices* through which love is communicated to others; either holding hands or embracing someone, is an expression of Love. It is crucial to fully comprehend that only one thing is certain and real, and that is *Love*. It is the only *real* thing that surrounds one's body at birth and upon death. *Love* is a *Divine Panacea* for all sickness in the mind; it's the essence of one's True Reality.

Personal values dictate the footprint of self-expression in day to day presentations. Be aware of the power of your words when you speak. All words are creative, do not take them lightly; they leave imprints in your world. What are the intentions, or thought processes behind your words? Are your inner thoughts creating good intentions, or do they have negative objectives? Use your voice to project love rather than hate. When a voice is used to cause hurt and pain, it is an enormous abuse of the creative breath. Expressions of love provide powerful spiritual nourishment to the Soul.

Words may be used to intentionally distort the truth to benefit oneself. Be ever vigilant in not allowing the thoughts of ego mind to direct your verbal expressions. Self-directed importance causes you to be oblivious to the needs of others. Can you hear the pain of others in words spoken or unspoken? It is the same voice as your own. Their pain is yours.

Constant fear of disapproval and un-acceptance represses and depresses self-expression. When you are frequently ridiculed or criticised, there is a reluctance to step forward and be heard, rendering one's voice powerless in expressing oneself. Do you have all kinds of creative ideas, but continue to self-sabotage because of fear of failure, success, and responsibility? Put a stop to the self-doubt which limits your potentiality.

Family influences play a major role in freedom of expression. Obligations and dependency on either your support or theirs, or needing their approval would greatly affect an ability to follow your dreams. A choice to nurture and support creative expressions in others, or to stomp on someone else's creative energy could have either a positive, or detrimental effect on your life's journey.

Do you use your voice to insult and degrade others, or project your own image of superiority, as a distraction from exposing your vulnerability and feelings of inferiority? This creates difficulty in connecting with others on an authentic personal level. Perhaps there is willingness to compromise the power of your voice by changing beliefs to conform to those of others, just to fit in, be accepted. Creating a continuous camouflage of deceitful stories makes it difficult to recognize what is true and what is false.

Having your life always in disarray, repeatedly dwelling on sickness or multiple problems, only serves the ego mind. Frequently questioning: "Why does this keep happening to me?" is a result of not accepting the fact that *nothing* actually happens *to* you, it happens *for* you. It's generally an alert, a siren, or a warning informing you that change is needed. Best heed these non-verbal voices or there will be bigger and more noticeable alarms if you continue down the same path.

Repeatedly lambasting or belittling yourself is as harmful as allowing others to demoralize and verbally abuse you. Self-defeating thoughts are responsible for a lack of positive choices. Believing that nothing will change, that the glass is always half empty, creates that reality in one's life. If one believes it, one will see it! Keeping one imprisoned in a pattern of negative behavior, serves to feed the ego rather than connecting to spirit.

Taking pleasure in disharmony and misfortune in other people's lives is a way to distract yourself from seeing your own failings, or stagnation of your life. Gossiping about others, sometimes even augmenting the stories, serves only to make oneself look more favorable. Your voice becomes a servant of the ego. Why do you lack self-respect, self-love, and self-worth? Constantly believing you are inadequate may cause you to fall victim to addictions, in attempt to suppress those thoughts. You are not aware of your True Reality and cannot appreciate your true value.

Fostering guilt because of an inability to express one's true feelings to loved ones becomes exasperated, as one gets older. It is crucial to come to terms with regrets, while there is an opportunity to say what needs to be said and make amends before it's too late. It takes a tremendous amount of courage to express love to others, when one has been starved of self-love or any other love. It is difficult to accept responsibility for one's own actions and requires tremendous fortitude to investigate and discover what problems lie deep within the mind.

Sometimes our religious beliefs give us a form of entitlement of spiritual intervention. We pray for help, not desiring to understand the part we may have played in a problem. Humanity is reluctant to clean up emotional messes. Prayers work only if personal responsibility is accepted and action is taken toward healing all wrong thinking, beliefs, and behaviors. All lacks and inadequacies are untruths needing to be understood and healed. Action is required, prayer is not enough.

An exhausting pattern of emotional discord contributes to the *draining* of energy and leaves one vulnerable to illness. When creative energy is stifled or stagnated, a zest for life is rapidly diminished, depression follows along with an inability to move forward. The body's voice is a significant tool for communicating truths; it is imperative to utilize your voice in assisting others to discover Truths of their Reality.

## Sixth Spiritual Disc

# MEMORY CACHE

## Remembrance:

*All are Guiltless, Pure Love, and Eternal.*
*The One Son of God - Christ Mind.*

## Spiritual Wisdom:

*Seek Spiritual Sight.*
*The Truth will set you Free!*

## Meditation:

*"The quiet of today will bless our hearts, and through them peace will come to everyone. Christ is our eyes today. And through His sight we offer healing to the world through Him, the Holy Son whom God created whole; the Holy Son whom God created one."* [11]

# Prayer:

*"I will not use the body's eyes today. Father, Christ's vision is Your gift to me, and it has power to translate all that the body's eyes behold into the sight of a forgiven world. How glorious and gracious is this world! Yet how much more will I perceive in it than sight can give. The world forgiven signifies Your Son acknowledges his Father, lets his dreams be brought to truth, and waits expectantly the one remaining instant more of time which ends forever, as Your memory returns to him. And now his will is one with Yours. His function now is but Your Own and every thought except Your Own is gone."* [12]

**Energy blocks caused by *wrong mindedness* manifest as sickness within the area of the body where the *Sixth Disc* is located. Parts of the body possibly affected:**

Brain, eyes, ears, nose, pineal and pituitary glands. Possible health issues: anxiety, headaches, various difficulties with the spine, paralysis, learning difficulties, neurological problems, multiple sclerosis, strokes, blood clots to the brain, brain hemorrhages and tumors, comas, mental, nervous and emotional breakdowns and disorders, Dementia and Alzheimer's disease, blindness, depression, schizophrenia, seizures, and deafness.

The **Sixth Memory Cache of *Light*** is situated in the middle of the forehead, commonly referred to the third-eye and spiritual sight. The ego's hold on the mind is now in jeopardy. It continues to dip into its bag of tricks to once again draw the mind back into illusion. It incessantly interjects controlling aspects into daily life. The ego mind is very much in a power struggle and control is its last tool for victory. If one recognized patterns of being a control freak, understand that it is ego's influence of the mind that is ruling that behavior.

The ego will continue to try to take the wheel, redirecting and enforcing its route down extreme and treacherous roads, causing a great deal of distress, fear, and pain. The body, the vehicle, will reflect the collateral damage sustained by consequent suffering in the mind. The ego mind is desperately trying to hold on to its control of the world because it realizes that its very existence is now in a precarious state.

Keeping the mind entangled in an attempt to control bodies and outside circumstances is crucial. Perhaps a more sinister mode of control comes under the guise of searching for perfection. This powerful ego tool is effective in sustaining and affirming separation. There are those who are winners and those who are not. Obsessively driven to achieve perfection; then, seeing it slip through one's grasp, can have devastating results if the bar is set too high and unattainable. Being a looser is greatly feared, resulting in disgrace and often abandonment; a shameful fall off an imaginary pedestal, in a futile attempt to hold on to the elusive crown of specialness.

Ego may utilize many psychic abilities of spirit communication and visions by projecting self-importance and aggrandizing the ego personality. It is quick to assume credit for any and all accomplishments of the mind, as it progressively draws the mind away from spirit and back into illusions. There is a furtherance of utilizing obsessive and continuous thinking, dragging out all its weapons of past hurts and possible future heart-breaks. It's best to humour the ego, so it is happy, inviting it along on the ride, but firmly let it know that it no longer is the driver of the experience.

A choice is made to continue a life ruled by fear, rather than submitting to Divine Faith for guidance. The irrational mind remains defiant, as belief in miracles and angels continue to challenge reason, even though many personal stories of Holy Visions and Spirit Communications have been recorded time after time. Ego mind demands proof before releasing its sure hold on the material world.

It's important to keep one's mind vigilant in constant remembrance of the Truth. Once the chains are loosened from the ego's emotional hold, the mind begins to see clearly though the illusions that keep it imprisoned within this world.

Choosing to be blind to a growing personal problem by avoiding it; hoping it will go away, never works. Obsessing and worrying needlessly about minor things, could lead to a situation that gradually morphs into a continuous and obsessive concern. Avoidance in addressing this kind of negative behavior progressively grows into a major problem, resulting in despair and a complete distortion of one's reality. It's important to firmly and strongly stand in one's personal power, but at the same time be flexible enough to bend with the stresses. Simply ask the Holy Spirit to choose for you, trust this will happen and just go with the flow.

Intuition is a source of spirit communication that can be used in day to day life. Knowing that Divine Guidance is constant in our lives, and by submitting to that energy gives one freedom from worry and responsibilities of multiple decisions every minute of every day. When one insists on personally controlling every detail in daily life, a life full of stress is created. If things don't work out according to plan, how does one react? Anxieties are caused by not accepting *what is* and wanting things to be different. With the many choices throughout the day, simply ask, "Holy Spirit choose for me!" You will be released from constant pressure of needing to focus on decision making.

Repetitive denial of responsibility in a situation, not being able to own and heal it, is a great detriment to spiritual progression. Keep trying to grasp the fact that one constantly projects unconscious pain and guilt onto others, they, in turn, serve as our mirror. It's imperative to implement *true forgiveness* in your life.

When you are able to recognize the common thread in constant chaos and emotional turmoil in your life as being yourself and accept personal responsibility, you will be placed on a direct path toward intense spiritual healing. Take responsibility for what you see and forgive yourself, release the emotional attachment and take the learning instead. Nothing happened in an illusion; no-one is guilty.

Does fear of failure prevent you from trying something different? Striving for perfection in every aspect of your life places monumental strain not only on yourself, but also on relationships. When one is disappointed in one's own accomplishments, there tends to be a projection onto others, expecting and demanding their perfection. Unfortunately this is a common projection on one's children, expecting them to fulfill the parents' failed dreams, making up for their own disappointments in life. Is doing your best not sufficient for your ego mind? Your True Self is perfect, follow the path to discover your True Reality.

Continually exerting control over every situation and imposing your superiority over others, serves to disguise your own weaknesses, vulnerabilities, and lack of inner control. A sick mind is incapable of true perfection, a completely healed mind is necessary before this state could be accomplished. A tremendous amount of guilt is suffered because of missed opportunities, life wasted, love wasted, and neglecting to provide loving support to oneself and others.

Controlling others by influencing and intimidating them creates slow and progressively debilitating diseases. This behavior serves to diverting the mind from a fact that one's own inner life is out of control. Chaotic situations are created, especially when others resist that control. A need to be needed drives an obsession of being responsible for everyone. When the ego's need for power and control are accepted and embraced, the consequences would be devastating and are reflected within a body.

With health issues such as a stroke, the result would be a total loss of mind's control, leaving the body vulnerable and dependant on others. As the body ages, reliance on others would be difficult to accept by someone who has control issues. The mind could be setting itself up for an extremely hard lesson. It may be a lesson of submitting to Divine Trust.

The ego convinces the mind, that war inflicting psychological and physical pain on others, or killing masses of people is okay. It is also acceptable to witness politically motivated actions, along with human created environmental disasters, causing tremendous human and animal suffering. When these events are no longer horrifying to the mind, with no desire to take action or responsibility, it causes a shrinking of Spirit within.

A moral compass in this world appears to be increasingly difficult to find. Witnessing extreme trauma, war, horrific accidents, death, and intense human suffering becomes repressed and suppressed in the unconscious mind. Ultimately, these events seem to take on a sense of acceptance and normalcy. Those kinds of issues are so opposite to what the True Self really is, which is Christ Mind, Pure Love, it is an attack on the Higher Self. This creates tremendous damage and a great potentiality for manifesting brain disease.

An unwillingness to entertain infinite possibilities temporarily suspends help and direction by Guides, Angels, and Higher Self. Spiritual sight can be greatly challenged and hindered. Change can be scary; it takes tremendous strength to be brave and step outside the box of comfort. Embracing the Truth that your Spirit and personality continues beyond the death of a body, releases countless chains that have bound you to this world for eons of time.

A journey through the *dark night of the Soul* leads to questioning pain that is a constant companion of this life. Questioning the value of this world comes when you find yourself in a constant state of self-defeat and progressively become despondent to life. There is a refocusing, a redirection of materialistic values to one of spiritual attainment. The greatest achievement to strive for is accessing spiritual wisdom and incorporating it into daily life.

A spiritual journey has many paths to the Truth. Some, however, seem to use the experience of searching, as a means with no end in sight. How committed are you? Travel if your must during your search, but you will find that the only journey that really needs to be taken is deep within your mind.

## SEVENTH SPIRITUAL DISC

# MEMORY CACHE

## Remembrance:

*You are the Observer, and the Observed.*
*The Silent Witness and the Witnessed.*
*You are the Thinker and the Thought.*
*The Cause and the Effect.*

## Spiritual Wisdom:

*Awaken to Truth!*
*All are One.*
*The Second Coming of Christ is You.*

## Meditation:

"Our Love awaits us as we go to Him, and walks beside us showing us the way. He fails in nothing. He the End we seek, and He the Means by which we go to Him."[13]

## Prayer:

"Father, our eyes are opening at last. Your holy world awaits us, as our sight is finally restored and we can see. We thought we suffered. But we had forgot the Son whom You created. Now we see that darkness is our own imagining, and light is there for us to look upon. Christ's vision changes darkness into light, for fear must disappear when love has come. Let me forgive Your holy world today, that I may look upon its holiness and understand it but reflects my own".[14]

This **Seventh Memory Cache of *Light*** is located directly in line with all others, it is at the crown of the body's head. Ego is no longer in the driver's seat, it is kicked to the back seat. Nevertheless, like all back-seat passengers, ego still attempts to give directions, continues to distract, confuse, and cause discord and disharmony. The fractured mind now chooses to move away from all attachments to bodies and materialistic things of this universe, toward becoming enlightened.

The mind begins to see through illusions of separation and understands that there is only a perception of separateness, it's only a mirage, a trick of the mind. There is an understanding of a truth that all others are merely fragmented parts of the same mind appearing as many, in different bodies and personalities, experiencing life from different perspectives. It is only the *belief* in the mind that it was fragmented and separated, which created this world.

The mind understands, embraces, and takes ownership of its own creation. There's a full understanding of projecting and mirroring, the importance of being vigilant in maintaining true perception all remaining days of one's life in this world. Remembrance of *True Reality* is among many gifts of wisdom in the *Memory Cache* of the final *Spiritual Disc*, the value of which is beyond description.

The mind through a body, teaches by example in expressing a fully enlightened life. It directs *Light* energy to assist humanity in taking steps forward on the intended path and encourages seeking knowledge of truth, which fulfills everyone's purpose of life in this world.

There is a full acceptance of a Truth that Jesus, our brother, was also a fractured part of the same mind. Jesus accessed the gift of remembrance and transcended the illusion. It is with Jesus' help that other fractured parts of the same mind will awaken, soon reunite, and be One in the Christ Mind, at Home with God in Heaven.

Life in this illusion will carry on until the appointed exit time, with full integration of an understanding of one's True Reality. The mind will experience this world with absolute awareness that it is not real, like watching a movie within which one has the leading role, or observing it as the Lucid Dream that it is. Of course, the script will now be changed to a loving existence with full emotional detachment, an awareness, and acknowledgement that there is only the Self, having an experience through many. Every day in one's life is now full of peace and joy, drawing others to desire the same. It truly would be *Heaven on Earth*!

An old Zen saying:
*Before enlightenment, chop wood and carry water.*
*After enlightenment, chop wood and carry water.*

## CONVERSATIONS WITH THE HIGHER SELF

*"Forgiveness is my function as the light of the world."*[15]
*"I am the light of the world. That is my only function.*
*That is why I am here."*[16]

Knowledge of the purpose of one's life, or the path one must travel to the Soul's designated destination, is embedded in the unconscious mind. Extracting that knowledge will entail processing denied and repressed memories full of intense and painful truths, bringing them to the surface to understand and heal. My purpose, your purpose, everyone's purpose is the same. We are all here for the same reason.

In 2011, during a hypnotic trance exercise, within which the unconscious mind was accessed, my Higher Self was guided by a series of questions, attempting to retrieve specific answers: *"What was I and what was the purpose of my life."* The initial question was, *"How do you appear?"*

The following responses are from my *Higher Self*:

*"I am creative not destructive. I'm aware of being what seems to be a diamond shape with different hues reflecting light all around me, a crystal of high vibrational energy. There is light reflecting and bouncing off everything around me, almost like I'm in a room full of mirrors or glass, light bouncing all over the place. I don't know what I am guided by, I'm guessing it's the sun, but I don't see the sun. I don't know where the light is coming from, it must be within me. The impulses that are operating are Light giving Love.*

*I'm channelling intense, positive, high vibrating, Light energy, which feels very light, other energies around me are very heavy. There is a force trying to guide me, but I am stuck in a vortex, stuck in one position, can't move because of blocks in others surrounding me. I see other energies trying to interact, but they've got blocks, they are dark and I'm bouncing off them. I'm buzzing and spinning, I can't seem to get through the barriers to move. I cannot seem to permeate their shells; I'm being contained.*

*I'm told my purpose is to bring Light into everything around me. To lighten the other energies and get rid of darkness; to project Light that would* reach as far as it can, so others could experience freedom. I need a new way of being, living and knowing, receptivity, open minds, open hearts - just opening up ways, freedom to be able to expand, and reflect further and further. Love needs to be communicated, that's Light - Unconditional Love! Patience is important and just to be, to set an example by what I am. It's okay to be different. It's okay to hold on to your Truth and not just follow the crowd.

There is a concern that I'm going to be on my journey alone because no one else is hearing, noticing or wanting what I have. Light may be blocked, that there could be barricades put up and I may not be able to permeate the barriers. I need to eliminate ignorance, lack of wisdom, fear of the unknown, and being different. Fear is a constant companion here and imprisons us in this world. I must be persistent, eliminate any thoughts of giving up. What needs to be integrated is open mindedness, receptivity, and creativity. More responsibilities of teaching and spreading wisdom needs to be delegated to others - more questions asked, more answers wanted and discovered, needing others on the same path, those who know of their Light.

I am being supported by wisdom that is innately within, a knowledge of needing to be persistent, patient, gentle, seeing Truth for what it is, and to realize that Truth is all around me and within me. My strengths are all that I Am, the power of Light and Love. My abilities are infinite, there's nothing that I lack; I am able to tap into the Truth of Essence, unconditional Love, Peace, and Joy. I am committed to being who I Am - True Love, the breath of Light expressing Love. I wish to elicit the responses of other energies to wake up and realize that they are brilliant Lights, beautiful and free. They are not dark energies; they are mistaken.

My long-term goals are not to give up, to be what I Am, to live by example, to be honest and truthful of what I Am. To assist others in remembering their True Reality. I desire that all have Freedom, Unconditional Love, Peace and Joy of Truth. It will be complete when I'm able to project Light throughout the whole world; it will be reflected back to me, all will accept it willingly lovingly. I will be what I Am when I leave this world, and the world will no longer exist. I am on the right path!

One's value is beyond any earthly value, it is a tremendous gift - the value of knowing one's True Reality - All that is - nothing could be more valuable. Priceless and Infinite!"

### Eight Spiritual Disc

# MEMORY CACHE

## Remembrance:

You are the Christ Mind, the Son of God!
Transcendence!

## Spiritual Wisdom:

True Self is: Incorporeal, Immutable, Infinite, Eternal, Omniscient, Omnipotent!

## Meditation:

*"Let us today behold earth disappear, at first transformed, and then, forgiven, fade entirely into God's holy Will.*

*Today we will accept our union with each other and our Source. We have no will apart from His, and all of us are one because His Will is shared by all of us. Through it we recognize that we are one. Through it we find our way at last to God."*[17]

## Prayer:

*"Father, our Name is Yours. In It we are united with all living things, and You Who are their one Creator. What we made and call by many different names is but a shadow we have tried to cast across Your Own reality. And we are glad and thankful we were wrong. All our mistakes we give to You, that we may be absolved from all effects our errors seemed to have. And we accept the truth You give, in place of every one of them. Your Name is our salvation and escape from what we made. Your Name unites us in the oneness which is our inheritance and peace. Amen.*

*Watch with me, angels, watch with me today. Let all God's holy Thoughts surround me, and be still with me while Heaven's Son is born. Let earthly sounds be quiet, and the sights to which I am accustomed disappear. Let Christ be welcomed where He is at home. And let Him hear the sounds He understands, and see but sights that show His Father's Love. Let Him no longer be a stranger here, for He is born again in me today."* [18]

The **Eight Memory Cache of *Light*** is located outside, above and beyond the body's limits, beyond Time and Space. One arrives at the finishing line, the last spiritual wisdom is graciously accepted, where time and space fades away and True Reality takes its place. It's merely a shift of perception and embracing pure Spiritual Vision that reveals the True Reality. The fractured mind has now integrated the Truth of an awakened Mind, the awareness of the Christ Mind, and transcended above the belief of existence in an illusionary body and universe.

As a part of the fractured mind, it ventured through an intense journey of discovery of Self. There is full acceptance and embracement of Truth that the One that has been absent for eons of time, and dearly missed, is none other than parts of the Self, able to reunite at last. One is consumed with tremendous happiness in knowing that the Self always was, and is still, at Home with God, the Christ Mind. Life on Earth was just a dream.

The mind discovers that the long search for the *One* of the *Light*, and long awaited and anticipated *Second Coming of Christ*, has come to an end. The *One* that has been searched for all along a length of time, has always been, the *Self - One - Christ Mind!*

## THE DREAM - REUNIFICATION OF SELF

As usual, after repetitively asking for spiritual guidance, a better understanding of many things that are foreign to the fractured mind's belief during existence in time and space, my Guides responded to me, once more, with a lucid dream.

**First Scene:** *I, Jeanette, was calling on a telephone, attempting to make a hair appointment with my hairdresser, by the name of* Jeanette. *The receptionist* *answered and I asked for the next available appointment with* Jeanette. *She was rather slow in responding apparently searching her appointment book for seemingly a long time. I was getting very impatient and asked her name, perhaps to make a complaint, I really don't know why I asked her name.*

*She replied, "My name is* Jeanette."

*I responded, "Don't you think it's odd that a* Jeanette *is speaking to a* Jeanette *regarding an appointment with a* Jeanette?" *The phone went dead.*

**Next scene:** *I was in my parent's retirement home, my dearly departed mother was sitting at the table, smiling patiently and lovingly while she watched me. My son walked through the door, and I, still confused, immediately relayed to him the story about the phone call that I just made. He hugged me, laughed, and said, "It's okay, just let it go."*

**Next scene:** *I found myself as part of a group of people in some sort of court yard, I was standing at the front of everyone facing a fenced area, an enclosure, in which there was a building with a closed door. The gate of the fence was wide open. I seemed to be waiting with great anticipation for an important announcement or a reveal.*

*A spokesperson stepped out of the building, leaving the door wide open and was about to speak, when a baby monkey ran out from behind him. At the same time, my* inner child *appearing to be about the same age as the monkey, seemed to move from within me and run eagerly and excitedly toward the baby monkey. Then, without any hesitation they quickly and intentionally wrapped their arms around each other, locking in an intense embrace full of passion and longing, as one would with a dearly missed loved one, who had been away a long, long time; reunited at last.*

## AWAKENING FROM THE DREAM

The impatient one making an appointment; inefficient receptionist; absent hairdresser; loving mother; kind son; anxious crowd; important spokesperson; observer; inner child; and baby monkey, the first fragmented part of the mind, first incarnated Self; are all fractured parts of the same one mind believing they were others. *All are just one mind dreaming of playing the roles of many.*

One mind is dreaming of having life experiences from different perspectives through a multitude of bodies. This dream included the usual other bodies with a variety of personalities, except there was an absence of different names, which greatly contributes to the appearance of separate beings. There is no separation; there never was. It was only a dream in one mind.

The first incarnation is reunited with the progressively awakening mind. Everyone is an expression of the same Self. They are all parts of the same sick mind, which believed that it separated from the one Christ Mind and the Source. All are One Mind, trying to wake up from the dream of separation, with an intense desire to be reunited, become whole again and at last awaken from the Dream!

# CHAPTER

# 23

# FOCUS ON END OF JOURNEY

*"The breeze of dawn has secrets to tell you.*
*Don't go back to sleep.*
*You must ask for what you really want.*
*Don't go back to sleep.*
*People are going back and forth,*
*where the two worlds touch.*
*The door is round and open.*
*Don't go back to sleep."*

## RUMI

Everyone's journey is different. Life takes many turns, many roads. What may be a wakeup call for some, may end up simply being a bump on the road for others. Grief was my breaking point; the *enough is enough* moment. I demanded to know why all pain existed. I could not understand how God could stand by and allow it, or, as some would suggest, intentionally create it. Nothing made sense to me; this world appeared foreign and ugly. Everyone's beliefs and behaviors brought such sorrow to me. I was observing a world of mind-controlled zombies, permanently imbedded in this insane space. I desperately desired an escape from all the ugliness of this world.

After much reading and meditating, a realization came to me that it was my mind that was controlled by all the fear, guilt, pain, and sorrow. I understood that I was looking in a mirror; what I was observing outside of me was inside of my mind. In an attempt to rid itself of unbearable mental anguish, it continually projected all the disharmony out into the world. I set out to learn how to heal all the conflict within me, so it would no longer dictate the kind of life and world I experienced. I wanted to get off the birth and death cycle permanently and was determined to learn how to accomplish it. I frantically searched and feverishly absorbed all information that would help me find a way out. Ten years later, I am happy to say, I see a flicker of *light*. I still have a distance to go, but there is a profound amount of clarity and a passionate focus on an anticipated destination.

*"I have lived on the lip of insanity, wanting to know reason, knocking on a door. The door opens. I've been knocking from inside"*. [1]

Seeking solutions in your imagined world, is an undertaking of a circular journey with no hope of ever finding an answer. The ego part of the mind which created the world of guilt, is always analyzing and investigating. The Higher Self understands the problems of trying to make sense of a convoluted existence. Inner knowledge is available when the mind becomes tired of *what is* and is ready to embrace a greater Truth.

I had been looking for answers outside of me for some time. Evidently that was a road I needed to travel. A slow accumulation of insights allowed for discernment and an ability to absorb crucial information. My astrological sun-sign is Capricorn - the goat who painfully, slowly, steadily, and assuredly climbs with every step firmly planted before the next step is taken on a precarious path. This was an undertaking of a journey that led me to the one true path to sanity.

We have been dealing with personal inner pain and seeking solutions, while continuing to think our inner pain is private, even though, we incessantly project it out into the world, for all to see. Nothing is private, separate, or different. We all experience the same pain. Mind's life's journey through a body while searching for spiritual enlightenment, ultimately brings it back to problems, answers, and solutions that were always within itself, just waiting to be retrieved, acknowledged, and embraced.

*"Therefore, seek not to change the world, but choose to change your mind about the world."* ²

The problems or solutions are not in the world, they are in the mind. Change your mind about the world and accept the Truth that it is only a *thought* in the mind. There is no such thing as *sin*; we all make mistakes; they are the means to life's lessons and consequential soul growth. If you change your beliefs about the world you see, understanding that no-thing was done by you or to you, you will project a forgiven and peaceful world.

Throughout a process of many life experiences, false beliefs have been ingrained, affirmed, and integrated as truths within the mind. As in religious cults, the mind has been programmed to accept a belief that may be difficult to change without deprogramming intervention.

There are countless others who have been fortunate enough to have been introduced to *A Course In Miracles*, have embraced its teachings and are actively integrating its lessons. A *Miracle* happens when there is an inner shift and a complete acceptance of the Truth of one's Reality. It is a form of deprogramming the mind, taking blinders off and entertaining other possibilities. Jesus' message within this book does not hurt, or harm anyone; it simply suggests a different way of looking at what we believe we see.

**"Remember only this; you need not believe the ideas, you need not accept them, and you need not even welcome them. Some of them you may actively resist. None of this will matter, or decrease their efficacy. But do not allow yourself to make exceptions in applying the ideas the workbook contains, and whatever your reactions to the ideas may be, use them. Nothing more than that is required."** ³

The course does not ask for any sacrifices, or harm you in anyway. It simply asks that you entertain the possibilities of its words and follow its ideas. Some people may have difficulty accepting the message; however, there would be a faint remembrance, or familiarity that keeps drawing one back to the teaching. Not everyone is ready for such a uniquely new perspective of this world, but it is the direction everyone will eventually choose to travel. All the time of the world is available to you; how much time are you wanting to take?

# WHO IS JESUS?

Jesus is a name, given to a man who was born and lived in an illusionary world. Just like each of us, Jesus was a fractured part of the same Christ Mind. He went through numerous life experiences in different bodies. Eventually, learning that love could overcome and heal all guilt, hate, and fear. He saw through the false and was able to see Christ's face in everyone. After discovering his True Reality, he successfully transcended the illusionary world.

Acknowledging the progressive and destructive ways of mankind, God asked Jesus to descend once more into the temptations and ugliness of this world, with the purpose of awakening humanity to the Truth. When He came back to teach us, He was fully aware that this world was an illusion. He knew of man's false beliefs and no longer identified Himself with any of them, was affected by them, or accepted them as Truth. Jesus needed to enter the illusionary world and use illusionary examples and explanations to assist humanity, the fragmented minds, to return to Self. It was only in body form, that He could teach others to follow His example of living.

Jesus was conceived and born the same way as every other human body. Contrary to religious beliefs, it was not a virgin birth. The Bible intentionally created the idea of a virgin birth to set Jesus apart from us; to make him a *God*; thus, giving Him a status, unattainable by mere mortals. To be believable and to be trusted, Jesus needed to be a body, so His message could be accepted by man. He knew he was in this world, but not of this world.

Jesus, as a body experienced the same trials and temptations we all face daily. He taught us how to overcome them all and find another way of living in this world. Jesus came as an example for mankind to follow and understand that everyone is his equal, his brothers and sisters. If He could do it, so could we. Most importantly, He came to help us understand the

Truth of who we are and how we might rise above this world. He was the Light guiding us home.

Jesus was aware of the tremendous power of a fully integrated and healed Mind. In fact, many of His miracles are attributed to the healed Mind's powerful capabilities. Several of His teachings, as they are portrayed in the Bible, were twisted and distorted to serve the purpose of controlling humanity. Most of Jesus' written words have been destroyed with the intention to keep humanity from ever knowing the Truth. Fortunately, some of these manuscripts were saved and buried deep in caves. As time goes on, they are being uncovered such as *The Dead Sea Scrolls*. Jesus' true teachings are now becoming available to mankind.

Once again in the 21[th] century, Jesus chose to reach us and teach us. He chose to channel his wisdom through a body by the name of Helen Schucman. His words were printed in a book called *A Course In Miracles*. Jesus tells us we are guiltless, we have not sinned, and we are forgiven for believing our bodies and this world are real. It is through forgiveness that we can break free from the relentless cycle of birth and death, as we continue to climb the evolutionary ladder to return to Self - the Christ Mind.

As each of us is awakened, we, too, can serve as the Voice of Jesus, calling to our brothers and sisters to awaken. Jesus reminds us He is our brother and that we are all eternally God's sons and daughters.

## WILL THERE BE A FINAL JUDGMENT?

*This is God's Final Judgment: "You are still My holy Son, forever innocent, forever loving and forever loved, as limitless as your Creator, and completely changeless and forever pure. Therefore awaken and return to Me. I am your Father and you are My Son."*[4]

The following information is from various past-life regressions, as well as those accumulated from personally regressed subjects, along with Spirit Communications. [5] When our bodies die, our Spirit along with its personality, transitions into a place called *Paradise*. Our Spirit is formless, colored energy with the color representing its evolutionary state. Our transitioned mind can present itself in any body of previous incarnations, creating any earthly forms that appear translucent and are experienced differently. The first level of *Paradise* is much like the earth plane, but without solid forms, or senses. There are at least 12 planes, the higher planes are occupied by the more progressively evolved Souls. It is composed of energy vibrating in different intensities; certainly higher vibrational intensities than the heavy, slow vibrational bodies of guilt on earth. It is a place for rest and healing, especially if the life experienced was one of extreme trauma. If life's choices were completely off balance with the True Self, there may be a necessity of a realignment of energy. There is colour energy healing as well as counselling.

No one judges us, we judge ourselves. When the body dies, we (the fractured minds) review the life lived, and we are assisted in seeing where and how things might have been done differently. Specifically, where we could have been forgiving and kinder to others. In our life review, we get to experience all the projected pain we inflicted on others. We experience it from the perspective of those on the receiving end of our wrath, we experience it all, as if we are them because we ARE them. We (fractured minds) take part in discussing how we might have chosen differently. With the help of Guides, intentions are set to do so, and we excitedly plan the next rebirth into the world thinking that it will be a piece of cake. There are classes and studies through which we attempt to learn forgotten wisdom in order to transcend our personality and remember our True Reality.

Nevertheless, when the mind re-enters under the veil of forgetfulness of the past and of its True Reality, it soon finds it is far from being an easy ride, once again. Sometimes it progresses and evolves closer to its True Self, sometimes it regresses. A step is taken forward or several steps backward, adding more essential and increasingly more difficult life experiences to the weaving of life's tapestry.

In this illusionary world, bodies and the universe are just that, an illusion. During our life experience, we must not judge others, in doing so we are simply judging ourselves. There are no *others*, there is only the Self believing it is many. An illusionary world holds nothing to judge. No-one did anything to hurt us, nor did we hurt anyone else; it's not possible for anything to be real in an illusion. It's like judging the actors within a movie and condemning them for having committed a crime. God never judges us. God is aware that we are asleep and dreaming a nightmare. Judgement only serves to chain us to the *time and space* world.

God's final judgement is the proclamation that the Son of God is sinless!

*"Holy are you, eternal, free and whole, at peace forever in the Heart of God. Where is the world, and where is sorrow now?"*[6]

## WILL THE WORLD END?

*"The world will end when its thought system has been completely reversed. Until then, bits and pieces of its thinking will still seem sensible. The final lesson, which brings the ending of the world, cannot be grasped by those not yet prepared to leave the world and go beyond its tiny reach."*[7]

Everyone's journey is different, but the destination is the same and the end is certain. Complete forgiveness of oneself and others for perceived infractions is crucial; the betrayals, abandonments, and rejections never happened. What you see out in the world is only what is happening in your own unhealed mind.

There really isn't anything to forgive. What needs to be forgiven is the fact that the mind believes the body and universe are real. During a time in my life when I was becoming completely disheartened, a voice said to me, "You cannot save the world you can only save yourself". One needs to take responsibility for oneself. It's important for the mind to change the way it sees the world, seeing it as the illusion that it is. This is a journey, undertaken by the separated mind within a mind; it desires to reconnect with itself and be whole again.

*"Here, with the journey's end before you, you see its purpose. And it is here you choose whether to look upon it or wander on, only to return and make the choice again."*[8]

We could have thousands of life experiences or more before the mind reaches a point of realization of a Truth that it was never fragmented or separated from the Source. Free will, the freedom to choose infinite number of times throughout life, is extremely significant. The mind's choices determine which paths are taken.

The fractured mind that contains your personality, can choose not to go through so many more experiences and decide to get on the main road to sanity sooner rather than later. Perhaps the mind will have had enough of the misery, and will choose to do the work required to get off this cycle. How many times will the mind need to approach the final curtain before it decides to take its final bow?

Through understanding how projection and mirroring works daily in our lives, the mind can implement learning, forgiveness, and healing. With the help of *other* bodies, the mind would become aware of where true forgiveness and healing is needed. Forgiveness of oneself and others, for believing the body and universe were real and completely understanding that *no-thing happened*, places one directly on the road *Home*.

How is your life working for you? Are you tired of pain, fear, guilt, sadness, and sickness? Jesus tells us we can save thousands of lifetimes by practising and living A *Course in Miracles*. Those who awaken sooner may choose to come back to assist those who are still determined to sleep walk through their lives, or they may choose to stay in Paradise and assist from there. Nevertheless, none of us will be whole until everyone or every separated self joins us.

*Heaven will continue to wait!*

## WHAT ABOUT OUR LOVED ONES?

What about our loved ones, do we leave them behind? Well, our loved ones, are also fragmented parts of the same sick mind. As with all fractured minds, our loved ones were projected outward to serve the purpose of avoiding the guilt within us. They are part of us and are never separated from us. Nevertheless, they will have to travel on a journey of self-healing and self-discovery. As we heal ourselves, so too, we will be healing future generations, quickening the process and eliminating a lot of unnecessary pain.

Once the separated parts have all integrated this Truth, the world will disappear and we will find ourselves together in the one Christ Mind, where we are right now, always were and will be forever. Can't get any closer than that! No more worrying, no more fears, and terrors of everyday life in this illusionary world. Everyone will be ONE, together, complete in Love, and embraced forever in the Heart of God.

It is like pulling your loved ones into your heart and lovingly enfolding them there, keeping them safe, completely enveloped in Love and Peace. It is the purest form of the most intense love you have always wished for, now with you eternally, never to be separated again. How would you like to feel that all the time? That truly would be Heaven. It is HEAVEN!

## WHAT IS RESURRECTION?

*"All living hearts are tranquil with a stir of deep anticipation, for the time of everlasting things is now at hand. There is no death. The Son of God is free. And in his freedom is the end of fear. No hidden places now remain on earth to shelter sick illusions, dreams of fear and misperceptions of the universe. All things are seen in light, and in the light their purpose is transformed and understood. And we, God's children, rise up from the dust and look upon our perfect sinlessness. The song of Heaven sounds around the world, as it is lifted up and brought to truth."[9]*

Resurrection is rising above the illusion, and completely embracing the Truth of one's Reality. The acceptance of Atonement, an act of love, is freeing yourself from the past, as you release the inner Light and absolutely commit to Spiritual Sight. It is a realization and acceptance that all are guiltless, limitless and Eternal - the Christ Mind.

The Holy Spirit, is the communication link between the fractured mind and God. The Holy Spirit utilizes the body as a learning tool, as a means of communication with other fractured minds. It is through this spiritual communication that the mind can be healed of all illusionary beliefs, such as pain, guilt, and sin. The mind will finally realize that there is no death, no fractured mind, and no world. With true vision the mind will rise out of this illusion, embrace Oneness, and awaken from this dream to find wholeness in the one *Christ Mind*. Its True Reality as an extension of the Creator's thought, the Son of God who always was, and always will be, Free and Eternal.

## HOW THE WORLD WILL END

*"When not one thought of sin remains, the world is over. It will not be destroyed nor attacked nor even touched. It will merely cease to seem to be."*[10]

Humanity is excitedly anticipating the second coming of Christ. Some believe He will descend from the sky, from a Heavenly place above and beyond the clouds. The fallacy of the second coming as being a physical event was made up by organized religions, imbedding the misconception that physicality was, indeed, a reality. Everyone is kept waiting for Christ while sustaining a belief that He is somewhere unfathomable and unreachable, but He will bestow Himself once more upon this world to save us. Erroneously, the mind, time over time, continues to believe it doesn't need to do, correct, or change anything just wait for redemption to be graciously bestowed upon this world.

*"The Second Coming is the time in which all minds are given to the hands of Christ to be returned to Spirit in the name of true creation and the Will of God."*[11]

We are never told that Christ literally *walks in our shoes*. We are all a part of the same mind, the Christ Mind. When all guilt is healed and no longer exists in the form of bodies, and all minds completely embrace the Truth of Reality, there will be an awakening from this dream. It is Christ's Truth that comes into the sick minds and heals it.

If we wish to hurry this along, we must each do our part. There is no free ride on someone else's back. Only you can heal yourself. It's important to work together to reach this end; we need each other. Remember the mind believes it is separated and until that belief system is obsolete, each fragmented part needs to do its own intense work of deprogramming, healing, and forgiving.

The awakened mind will adopt the Truth that it never was separated and always was the *One Whole - Christ Mind*, at which time, the universe will collapse onto itself and return to where it came from, back to the *nothingness* it always was. Just a *thought!*

**"There is no death because the Son of God is like his Father. Nothing you can do can change Eternal Love. Forget your dreams of sin and guilt, and come with me instead to share the resurrection of God's Son. And bring with you all those whom He has sent to you to care for as I care for you."**[12]

Only when the mind is fully awaken from this dream, united and one in the Christ Mind, will it find itself, where it was all along the whole length of Time, at Home with God. The long-anticipated arrival of the Son of God will now be over. You are the One you have been looking and waiting for! Rise up and remember that **You** are **the Son of God!**

The Christ Light will forever shine with Love through everything because that's all there ever was and ever will be.

**"And so the journey which the Son of God began has ended in the light from which he came.**[13]

*"And now we say Amen. For Christ has come to dwell in the abode You set for Him before time was, in calm eternity. The journey closes, ending at the place where it began. No trace of it remains. Not one illusion is accorded faith, and not one spot of darkness still remains to hide the face of Christ from anyone. Thy Will is done, complete and perfectly, and all creation recognizes You, and knows You as the only Source it has. Clear in Your likeness does the light shine forth from everything that lives and moves in You. For we have reached where all of us are one, and we are home, where You would have us be."* [14]

# NOTES

A note on reading Course references:

All references are given for the Second Edition of the Course, and are listed according to the numbering in the course, rather than according to page numbers. Each reference begins with a letter, which denotes the particular volume or section of the Course and its extensions (T = Text, W = Workbook for Student, M = Manual for Teachers, C = Clarification of Terms.) After this letter comes a series of numbers, which differ from volume to volume:

T,P, or S - chapter.section.paragraph: sentence; e.g., T-7.VIII.2:2-3

W-part (I or II), lesson.paragraph:sentence; e.g., W-pII.10.5:1-3

M or C - section.paragraph: sentence; e.g. M-14.2: 10-11

Words in parentheses are my own.

---

Works now Public Domain:

http://www.publicdomainsherpa.com/public-domain-books.html

https://www.smithsonianmag.com/arts-culture/first-time-20-years-copyrighted-works-enter-public-domain-180971016/

https://law.duke.edu/cspd/publicdomainday/2019/

Rumi; D.H.Huxley; Edgar Allan Poe; Mahatma Gandhi; Hermes - Kahlil Gibran;

Kybalion: www.kybalion.org Bodhidharma - U.G. Krishnamurti: reprinted in accordance with Mr. Krishnamurti's copyright policy: "My teaching, if that is the word you want to use, has no copyright. You are free to reproduce, distribute, interpret, distort, garble, do what you like, even claim authorship, without my consent or the permission of anybody.

Introduction
1    ACIM W-pII.326:2

Chapter Three
1    Edgar Alan Poe
2    Mahatma Gandhi

Chapter Four
1    Rumi
2    Rumi
3    Gautama Buddha
4    https://www.britannica.com/science/unconscious

Chapter Six
1    Gautama Buddha
2    http://www.themonkeytrap.us/about-the-monkey-trap

Chapter Seven
1    ACIM W-pI.92.2
2    https://www.linkedin.com/pulse/nothing-solid-everything-energy-Scientists-explain-world-djurisic
3    Rumi
4    https://www.britannica.com/science/subatomic-particle
5    httsp://education.jlab.org/ga/how-much-of-an-atom-is-empty space?

6    Mahatma Gandhi

7    https://www.aoa.org/patients-and-public/resources-for-teachers/how-your-eyes-work

8    https://www.britannica.com/science/human-sensory-reception

9    https://www.psychologytoday.com/us/blog/think-well/201906/does-consciousness-exist-outside-the-brain

## Chapter Eight
1    ACIM W-pI.92.1:4-5

2    Author Unknown

## Chapter Nine
1    ACIM W-pI.R.V.9:3-7

2    Rumi

## Chapter 10
1    https://edgy.app/paralle-univers-ideas-explained

2    https://www.brandeis.edu/now/2018/november/the take-podcast-hologram.html

3    Bodhidharma

4    https:www.cbc.ca/nature of things/episodes/myth-or-science-of-our-senses

5    Rumi

6    https://www.ctvnews.ca/business/payless-tricks-social-media-influences-into-paying-600-for-20-shoes-1.4199050

## Chapter Eleven
1    ACIM T-2.1.3:5-7

2    Edgar Allan Roe

3    ACIM T-2.1.4:5-9

4    https://faculty.washington.edu/smchen/320/cave.htm

## Chapter Twelve
1    ACIM T-30.IV.5:1-3;8:14 -15

2    ACIM T-8.VII.7:1- 4

3    https://archive.org/stream/StephenHawkingABriefHistoryOfTime/Stephen+Hawking+A+Brief+History+Of+Time djvu.txt

4    Hermes

5  Rumi

6  ACIM W-pII.13.1:1-3

7  ACIM Preface, - page vii

8  ACIM T-Intro.2:1-4

9  Kahlil Gibran

10 Rumi


## Chapter Thirteen

1  ACIM T-28.V.4:2 -9

2  ACIM T-28.II.4:2-3;7:1;11:1

3  ACIM T-27.VIII.6:2-3

4  https://www.newscientist.com/article/mg20327246-600-13-more-things-antimatter-mystery/

5  https://ihavenotv.com/series/how-the-universe-works

6  https://www.nationalgeograpic.com/science/space/dar-matter/

7  ACIM T-27.VIII.7:2-7

8  ACIM C-6.4:1-3

9  ACIM C-6.3:4-9


## Chapter Fourteen

1  ACIM T-20.VIII.7:3-5

2  The Kybalion

3  ACIM W-pI.128.2:1

4  ACIM T-23.II.18:8-9

5  CIM W-pI.129.2:1-6

6  https://m.poets.org/poetsorg/poem/children-1


## Chapter Fifteen

1  ACIM W-pII-333.1:1-4

2  ACIM W-pII.249.1:1-7

3  ACIM T-18.V.6:1-2

4  ACIM W-pI.198.2:1-3

5  ACIM W-pII.265.1: 1-3

6  ACIM W-pII.335.1:1-7

7  ACIM WpI.140.10:4

## Chapter Sixteen

1   Gautama Buddha

## Chapter Seventeen

1   ACIM T-24.1.4:2-5

2   Mahatma Gandhi

## Chapter Eighteen

1   ACIM T-29.VII.2:1-2; 4-5

2   ACIM T-13. intro.2:2-10

3   Young blood company stops unproven anti-aging treatment after FDA https:/ www.cnn.com/2019/02/19/health/plasma-infusion-young-blood-fda..../ index.html and https://clinicaltrials.gov/ct2/show/NCT02803554?term= youg+plasma

4   ACIM W-p1.73.10:2-3

5   U.G. Krishnamurti

6   ACIM T-27.VIII.3:1- 6;4:1-5

7   ACIM W-pII.260.1:1-6

## Chapter Nineteen

1   ACIM T-5.V:5-6

2   ACIM W-pII-5.1:1-3

3   How Psychology Combats False and Self-Limiting Beliefs: https://positive psychology.com/false-beliefs/

4   Mahatma Gandhi

## Chapter Twenty

1   ACIM W-pI.136.2:1-5

2   https://www.uofmhealth.org/health-library/hw180537

3   ACIM W-pI.136.7:3-4

4   ACIM W-pII.5.4:1-5

## Chapter Twenty - One

1   ACIM W-pI.190.5:1-6

2   https://www.dailymail.co.uk/health/article-1219995/Believe-lungs-weeks-old- -taste-buds-just-days-So-old-rest-body.html

## Chapter Twenty - Two

1    ACIM W-pI.110; pI.120.2:2-3

2    ACIM WpI-130.8:5-6; W-pII.272.1:1-8; 2:1-2

3    ACIM W-pII.253.1:1-6

4    ACIM W-pII.252.2:1-2

5    ACIM W-pI.49; 60.4:1-5

6    ACIM W-pI.183.3:1-6

7    ACIM W-pII.334.1:1-6

8    ACIM W-pI.121.10:1-4; 11:1-4; 12:1-3; 13:1-7

9    ACIM WpI.118.2:2

10   ACIM W-pI.R.V.2:1-6; 3:1-6

11   ACIM W-pII.270.2:1-3

12   ACIM W-pII.270.1:1-6

13   ACIM W-PII.302.2:1-3

14   ACIM W-pII.302.1:1-7

15   ACIM W-pI.62.Heading

16   ACIM W-pI.61.5:3-5

17   ACIM W-pII.326.2; W-pII.329.2:1-4

18   ACIM W-pI.184.15:1-9; pII.303.1:1-6

## Chapter Twenty Three

1    Rumi

2    ACIM T-21.Intro.1:7-8

3    ACIM W-intro.9:1-5

4    ACIM W-pII.10.5:1-3

5    The three Waves of Volunteer's and the New Earth; Between Death and Life - Dolores Cannon; Memories of the Afterlife; Journey of Souls - Michael Newton, Ph. D.; Many Lies, Many Masters; Miracles Happen - Brian L. Weiss, M.D.

6    ACIM M-15.1:11-12

7    ACIM M-14.4:1-3

8    ACIM T-19.IV.D.i.10:7-8

9    ACIM M-28.4:1-8

10   ACIM M-14.2:10-12

11   ACIM W-pII.9.3:3
12   ACIM C-5.6:9-12
13   ACIM W-pII.249.1:7
14   T-31.VIII.12:1-8

# RECOMMENDED READING RESOURCES

--*A Course in Miracles, Foundation for Inner Peace* Website (foundation for Inner Peace): http://www.acim.org Highly recommend this book, which through the 669-page Text, 488-page Workbook for Students, and 92-page Manual for Teachers, brings tremendous clarity, learning, and healing opportunities through a path of recalling forgotten knowledge. Resulting in a release from the birth and death cycle. A True Awakening.

--Allen Watson and Robert Perry - *A Workbook Companion - Volume I and II, - Course in Miracles*

--Wapnick, Gloria, and Kenneth Wapnick, Ph.D. - *The most commonly Asked question About A Course in Miracles.*

--Wapnick, Kenneth, PH.D., and Gloria Wapnick. - *Awaken from the Dream;*

*A Presentation of - A Course in Miracles,* second edition.

--Wapnick, Kenneth, PH.D.: *A Vast Illusion - Time According to A Course in Miracles,* second edition.
*Ending Our Resistance to Love*: The Practice of A Course in Miracles.
*The Healing Power of Kindness,*: Releasing Judgment
*The Message of A Course in Miracles*: All are Called, Few Choose to Listen
*Forgiveness and Jesus:* The Meeting Place of A Course in Miracles and Christianity

*Absence from Felicity*: The Story of Helen Schucman and Her Scribing of A Course in Miracles.
*The Journey Home: "The Obstacles to Peace"*: in A Course in Miracles
*Fifty Miracle Principles of A Course in Miracles.*
*Glossary-Index for A Course in Miracles*

--<u>Renard, Gary R</u>: - *The Disappearance of the Universe*; Straight Talk About Illusions, Past Lives, Religion, Sex, Politics and the Miracles of Forgiveness.
*Your Immortal Reality*: How to Break the Cycle of Birth and Death.

--<u>Tolle, Eckhart</u>: *The Power of Now*: A Guide to Spiritual Enlightenment.
*Stillness Speaks*
*A New Earth*: Awakening to Your Life's Purpose

--<u>Gary Zukav:</u> *Soul Stories*
.....*The Seat of The Soul*

--<u>Deepak Chopra</u>: *How To Know God*
*Power Freedom and Grace*
*Spontaneous Fulfillment of Desire*

--<u>Dr. Wayne W. Dyer</u>: Inspiration - *Your Ultimate Calling*

--<u>Chelsea Quinn Yarbro</u>: *Messages from Michael*

--<u>Katie, Byron, with Stephen Mitchell</u>: *Loving What Is:* Four Questions That Can Change Your Life.

--<u>Caroline Myss</u>: *Sacred Contracts:* Wakening Your Divine Potential
*Anatomy Of The Spirit*
*The Creation of Health*

--<u>Nauk Sanchez and Tomas Vieira</u>: *Take Me to Truth*- Undoing the Ego

--<u>Willigis Jager</u>: *Search For The Meaning Of Life*: Essays and Reflections on the Mystical Experience.

--<u>Michael Talbot</u>: *The Holographic Universe*

--<u>Robert Perry</u>: *Path of Light,* Stepping into Peace with A Course in Miracles

--<u>Paul Elder</u>: *Eyes of an Angel,*

--<u>Colin Tipping</u>: *Radical Forgiveness*

--<u>Esther and Jerry Hicks</u>: *Ask and It Is Given*

--<u>Delores Cannon</u>: *Between Death & Life*
*Jesus and The Essenes*
*The Convoluted Universe*
*The Three Waves of Volunteers and The New Earth*

--<u>David Icke</u>: *Infinite Love is the Only truth, Everything Else is Illusion*

--<u>Charles Ferris</u>: *Twelve Dimension*

--<u>Michael Newton</u>, PH.D.: *Journey of Souls - Case Studies of Life Between Lives*
*Memories of the Afterlife - Life Between Lives*

--<u>Brian L. Weiss, M.D. and Amy E. Weiss, M.C.W.</u>: *Miracles Happen - The Transformational Healing Power of Past-Life Memories;*
*Many Lives, many Masters*

--<u>Penney Peirce</u>: Frequency - *The Power of Personal Vibration*

--<u>Dannion Brinkley with Paul Perry</u>: *Saved By The Light*

--<u>Rosemary Altea</u>: *A Matter of Life & Death- Remarkable True Stories of Hope and Healing*

--<u>Todd Burpo with Lynn Vincent</u>: *Heaven is for Real*

--<u>Crystal McVea and Alex Tresniowski</u>: *Waking up in Heaven*

--<u>James Van Praagh</u>: *Talking to Heaven*

--<u>Louise L. Hay</u>: *You Can Heal Your Life*

--<u>William E. Williams</u>: *Unbounded Light - The Inward Journey*

--<u>Dr Brenda Davies</u>: *Journey of the Soul*

--<u>Paul Ferrini</u>: *The Bridge to Reality*
--<u>Leo Hartong</u>: *Awakening To the Dream*
--<u>Mark Schatzker</u>: *The Dorito Effect*

AUTHOR'S WEBSITE:

www.jeanetteshewchukauthor.com

www.jeanetteshewchuk.com - blog

Face book Page:

Healing Grief & Life's Emotional Pain - A Journey to Enlightenment

Printed in the United States
By Bookmasters